Sex in Society

Also by ALEX COMFORT:

Verse

A Wreath for the Living. *Routledge.* 1943.
Elegies. *Routledge.* 1944.
And All But He Departed. *Routledge.* 1951.
Haste to the Wedding. *Eyre & Spottiswoode.* 1962.

Novels

No Such Liberty. *Chapman & Hall.* 1941,
The Almond Tree. *Chapman & Hall.* 1943.
The Powerhouse. *Routledge.* 1944.
On This Side Nothing. *Routledge.* 1948.
A Giant's Strength. *Routledge.* 1952.
Come Out to Play. *Eyre & Spottiswoode.* 1961.

Essays

Art & Social Responsibility. *Grey Walls Press.* 1947.
Barbarism & Sexual Freedom. *Freedom Press.* 1948.
Darwin and the Naked Lady. *Routledge.* 1961.

Textbooks

First-year Physiological Technique. *Staples.* 1948.
Authority & Delinquency in the Modern State. *Routledge.* 1950.
The Biology of Senescence. *Routledge.* 1956.

ALEX COMFORT

Sex in Society

THE CITADEL PRESS
SECAUCUS, N.J.

HQ
31
.C6
1963 /59,950

Second American printing, January 1975
Third American printing, February 1975
Copyright © 1963 by Alex Comfort
Published by Citadel Press
A division of Lyle Stuart, Inc.
120 Enterprise Ave., Secaucus, N.J. 07094
Manufactured in the United States of America
ISBN 0-8065-0064-6

Contents

Sex in Society

Introduction

THE extent, popularity, and emotive tone of the literature of sexual behaviour are sufficient warnings to anyone who is invited to add to it, and I have done so reluctantly. While it is true that full public discussion and information is essential in this field, it is also true that the task of deflating the emotional currency of sex is equally important. The undermining of an older false-modesty has unfortunately not yet reduced the tension that exists in the mind of the public or its scientific advisers, and zealots who put forward theories of sex as a *mystique* or a transcendent human activity have already done a great deal to obscure its real place as a single, if important, part of a general pattern of human social activities.

When I first wrote this book (in 1950) I had in mind an audience chiefly drawn from the various types of 'social worker'. In rewriting it I have removed some ill-judged remarks and put in some new ideas and information. It would be disingenuous to present any book which meddles so extensively with ethics and social organization as a dispassionate survey of facts, particularly when both the facts and their significance are highly contentious. It is not a textbook for any social diploma, but rather a sequence of argument, embodying the deductions which the author has drawn, under the influence of his own prejudices, from the facts as they appear to be. I have tried to compensate for this by including references, which those who value their objectivity should look up. The society referred to as 'us' and 'ours' is, if not further particularized, that of contemporary London, and conclusions about other places should not be drawn rashly from it. I have deliberately hedged, so far as possible, on issues where the facts are not yet sufficiently known to support a distinct opinion. Wherever an unsupported generalization occurs, it should be prefaced by the

7

reader with the words, 'He would, given the time and space, be prepared to make out a case that, etc.' Since only obsessional readers are likely to attempt to cover all the references, I have taken the liberty of marking with an asterisk those which appear to me to be of the greatest general interest.

A. C.

London, 1962.

I

The Scope and Purposes of Sexual Sociology

THE study of human sexual behaviour is one of the most important and instructive branches of the study of man. It is not the province of any single science, but overlaps into the fields of psychology, physiology, social anthropology, and ethics. This multiple interest adds, in many ways, to the difficulty of an already difficult field. The word 'sexology', which has been coined as a generic name for sexual study, has acquired the particular meaning of clinical instruction in sex hygiene, which is no part of the intention of this book. Approaches in the past by way of anthropology, physiology, and psychoanalysis have all contributed much to knowledge, but under present conditions our view of sexual problems and institutions needs a wider basis, covering all existing sources of information – the viewpoint of what we may call human biology.

Scientific estimates of the importance of sexual studies have varied widely with the prevailing attitudes of the societies in which they have been formed. Early in the century most research in Europe was focused on the relationship between atypical sexual behaviour and mental disorder, and the teaching of Freud gave a considerable impetus to sexual psychopathology. The emphasis in recent work is different. Sociologists are interested in sexual behaviour for two main reasons: because of its importance in the psychology of the individual, sexuality and institutions and beliefs associated with it are among the most useful points of approach to the study of a society; and because of its relationship to the structure of the family, the pattern of sexually acceptable conduct plays a large part in perpetuating social attitudes and in the formation of individual character. Apart from this interrelationship, problems

9

of sexual conduct and education have acquired a growing practical importance in all forms of social work, which has largely outstripped both the state of public knowledge and the information of doctors and social workers themselves.

The nutrition and eating habits of a society or an individual can be studied objectively in civilized countries, without any violent reaction being evoked, either by the study or its findings. Societies have existed, and still exist, in which equally dispassionate study of sexual behaviour is possible, but it is historically impossible to conduct such a study in contemporary English or American societies. Sexual studies have therefore been and still are in a uniquely difficult position. While most people are familiar through conversation with the dietary habits of their neighbours and their own social group, the knowledge which the average Englishman or American possesses about the sexual behaviour of his fellows is limited to a degree. For several centuries open discussion of some forms of sexual conduct has been restricted or prohibited by convention and by religious belief, and the scope of this prohibition widened during the early nineteenth century to include almost all aspects of the subject. The emotional overtones of sex, and its place in the censorship of conduct and speech, have steadily grown with the growth of civilization, but this process reached an exceptional peak in the middle Industrial period of English urban society, and the disapproval of sexual study lasted until the advent of psychoanalysis. The growth of scientific knowledge since that time has not yet succeeded in reducing the emotional tension which exists in the minds both of the public and of the scientist whenever sexual conduct is discussed.

The results of this process have been multiple, and they all tend to increase the difficulties of intelligent study. The state of public information on sexual matters remains poor, and ignorance of elementary physiology and of average human conduct increases the individual's difficulties: the scientist frequently has to contend with a complete absence of unbiased data, with a large measure of social disapproval, and with the risks of an emotionally loaded subject. In a society that has long regarded sexuality as shameful, and its manifestations as dan-

10

gerous and hostile actions, it is impossible to set up rational standards of investigation overnight. The easing of the restraints of Victorianism has led to an equally irrational reaction in literature and thought, to philosophies that treat sex as a *mystique*, and to anxiety about it of a different kind. Social psychologists are no more immune from this type of group reaction than others, and the whole field retains a fatal attraction for psychopaths, which is reflected in much which has been written on sexual matters and presents a serious problem in the selection of reliable marriage-guidance and psychiatric workers.

Quite apart from this, it has also meant that we still know a great deal less about the detailed physiology and variation of human mating behaviour than about that of the economically important domestic animals. The need to know more does not spring only from idle curiosity – the use of such knowledge will be fully recognized by anyone who has tried to get sensible advice over some minor difficulty of sexual technique, or, for that matter, to give it. Much which has been written about such matters over generations of medical books proves on critical examination to be sheer moonshine: a well-intentioned counsellor, no less than his patient, still cannot always get detailed statistical studies on which to base his advice – or cannot get anything like the volume of evidence which would be available if the inquiry dealt, say, with diet. Often he will settle for an answer in terms of his own sexual experience; unfortunately, the one thing which does emerge from recent work is that human sexual needs, responses and capacities are immensely variable, and what one man or woman has learned by experience, often with a single partner, simply does not apply to many others. And in the absence of facts, poppycock of every kind flourishes.

Our society normally restricts the term 'sexual' to activities and relationships which have to do with reproduction, or which are associated with the reproductive system. One of the most important changes in scientific thought since the coming of psychoanalysis has been the recognition that this classification is artificial. There is no very clear dividing line between personal relationships which are 'sexual' in the restricted sense and those which are not. Savage societies, and particularly those which have not recognized the connection between sexual intercourse and conception, appear to have had difficulty in distinguishing between reproductive and non-reproductive relationships. In animals, relationships between sexually mature adults are all potentially reproductive, the various other forms of social behaviour being largely determined by the existence of cyclical patterns of activity. Man has recognized the basic similarity of impulse which underlies family life in its non-sexual aspects and mating-behaviour by developing a strong social and individual fear of incest – possibly for biologically-patterned reasons which we shall encounter presently. This fear has played a large part in determining the institutions of many societies, and is very deeply rooted in the individual mind – in our time it has done much to obscure the fact that the relationships which exist between parent and child, no less than those between adults of opposite sexes, spring from a common impulse and a common group of experience. This identity and continuity were asserted by Freud, but the restricted current meaning of the term 'sexual' has led to a great deal of misunderstanding by readers of his work.

What Freud did in fact show was that a large and highly important section of human mental behaviour is a phylogenetic expansion of sexuality, and that in the course of this development one particular sexual mechanism, the Oedipus complex, in which sexuality is associated with instinctive anxiety, has become critical in determining the structure of the human mind. It may, indeed, have been the chief biological force in the evolution of humanness. It is this key place in the economy of man which accounts for the unique significance which sexuality has for us, and its association with anxiety accounts for our odd preoccupation with it.

The observational study of sexual behaviour has come to cover two fields – the field of individual relationships, their dynamics and their modifications, and the field of specifically reproductive behaviour – and the two shade into one another without any very definite boundary. The emotional content of of our attitude toward sex influences both fields, although we are conscious of it chiefly in the second. Besides the collection and interpretation of facts, sexual sociology is increasingly forming and influencing the standards and patterns of individual conduct. This is a function it neither desires nor is able to repudiate. The formative influence of science on ethics is, on almost all counts, a beneficial one. Facts are not ethical principles, but they tend to form or revise our moral ideas by making it harder to believe nonsense.

It would be intensely interesting to know how far survey studies exhibit the interference paradox – how far their conduct and publication alter the pattern which is being observed. This is a general problem in cases where scientists collect and publish factual information about social attitudes – sex behaviour is probably not one of the most easily affected, for it seems to be fixed fairly early, and to be rather stable. On the other hand, the main value of survey studies at the social level is that they expose the discrepancy between what society pretends and what people do, and this exposure will probably influence the conduct of some, if only by reassuring the timid that what they would do if they dared, their outwardly conformist neighbours are doing in fact. If it is statistically established that fifty per cent of the strenuously upright are really no better than the rest of us, public morality begins by that very realisation to be brought back to the basis of real behaviour. The main effect of knowledge, then, is likely to be a gain in candour and realism, and the good done by letting in so much fresh air is likely to outweigh the possibility that a few may catch cold.

The situation of sexual study in Western Europe is still very much what the situation of nutrition and dietetics would be in a society that traditionally attached magical and emotional significance to what it ate, and to the preparation of food, though it varies widely from country to country. One can imagine the difficulties of such a study if menus and photographs of meat and vegetables were surreptitiously sold on seaside piers, and a taste for pies or fried fish was so inacceptable to society that a patient would admit it only under pressure and to a psychiatrist. In such a society malnutrition would be frequent and, in the absence of accurate data, very hard to treat; and the repressed preferences of the investigators would perpetually intrude into their work. Upholders of dietary morality, having failed to retain their hold on the superstition of the public, would devote much time to proving the deleterious effects of certain foods, and attempts at scientific assessment of such effects would be regarded with great hostility and resentment.

There is, of course, no strict analogy between the two conditions, but social insects have expanded their feeding behaviour rather as man has expanded his sexual behaviour, so that in ants and termites it has generated a vast and complicated system of social living and specialization. Such insects, if they were rational, might be as liable to superstition and disturbance in the discussion of diet as man is in the discussion of sex. This would be still more likely if they were obliged to go through a critical period of development in which food was associated with anxiety, and this anxiety had later to be repressed. Sexual attitudes and prejudices accordingly play a far more important part than diet in determining the form of society and the attitude of the individual, and in the ethical basis of society. They have also a unique unconscious significance for the individual – in fact, when extreme anxiety or concern over a dietary matter appears in man, it is usually cover for an unconscious disturbance of sexuality. But both are open to the same methods of study, and the scientist has to ask whether the fact that he does not find himself involved in ethical arguments when he discusses nutrition has any bearing on his attitude to sexual behaviour. In this field it is almost impossible to keep up the pretence of dispassionate inquiry into facts, apart from their interpretation. Medicine can decide by study whether a given food or a given sexual practice is physically harmful, but the ill effects of most forms of sexual behaviour that are regarded as unhealthy depend almost wholly on the fact that they are feared or detested by society on moral grounds, and on the feelings of guilt they evoke in the individual. Science is therefore forced to decide how far it is going to adhere to rational criteria in dealing with religious or social systems of conduct. In writing a book of this kind, some such decision must be reached. Every new fact is a comment on the reasonableness of current attitudes. The view put forward here is based on the form of rationalism and humanism which seems to the author closest to the general spirit of experimental science: that no form of sexual behaviour can be regarded as inacceptable, sinful, or deserving of censure unless it has demonstrable ill effects on the individual who practices it, or on others.

In fact, in the medical literature of sex we can notice a steady and directional movement, from Sinibaldus's seventeenth century *Geneanthropeia*,[1] the fount and origin of nearly all the most persistent nonsense about reproductive and sexual matters in the European tradition, through Venette's popularizations which circulated in the eighteenth century, to the textbooks of 1900 and even later. In all this tradition the concern of the writers was far less to ascertain facts than to uphold existing beliefs by exhortation and threats; in other words, medicine was helping most shamelessly to work the oracle for convention. Every deviant form of sexual behaviour, judged by the standards of the religio-cultural convention, was not only morally wrong, but, in case that failed to check it, ruinously unhealthy as well. The case of masturbation is perhaps the most typical – almost every physician from Sinibaldus down must have practised it, and any physician could have ascertained, by a straw poll of his former schoolmates, that they had done the same. Yet generation after generation of medical writers descanted on its ghastly and wholly imaginary ill effects – and indeed, succeeded in producing most of them in suggestible or anxious readers. The only major dissentient was John Hunter, who found it much less dangerous than intercourse with heavily-infected prostitutes, and was abused as a corrupter of youth for saying so publicly. The same applies to almost all other sexual activities – including normal intercourse in marriage, a dangerous business, which was grudgingly admitted provided there was not too much of it – the risk of 'excess' being always to hand to prevent over-enthusiastic enjoyment.

In this, of course, medical men only echoed the anti-sexual tone of the 'overt culture' – meaning the moral posture of society, contrasted with what it does in the privacy of its own home. With the growth of knowledge and of rationalism the ground shifted, no less in medical than in religious and moralistic writings. What was sinful and leading to damnation became deadly and productive of cancer and insanity; then unhealthy, and a cause of muddy complexion, poor wind and bags under the eyes – and finally 'immature' and a sign of low moral fibre, if not of neurosis. Many sexual manifestations are indeed examples of what psychiatrists term regression – but so are smoking, praying, swearing, playing jokes or football, and going to the pictures – to say nothing of the fantasy pleasures we derive from art and literature. Shorn of all immaturities we would be equally shorn of most of our motivation.

Ours is the first generation which has decided to find out what real effects, if any, sexual practices have upon health, and with what states of mind and body they are correlated, by the method of counting heads. It was certainly high time, but one cannot be too sanguine that the availability of the facts will shake the deep-seated need of some medical and psychological moralists at least to find reservations upon this newly-discovered prospect of sex without artificially-stimulated anxiety. In any case time will tell.

Thus, for example, we find Lorand[2] writing in 1925, in precisely the tone of Sinibaldus 'Too frequent sexual intercourse may soon sap the vitality of the glands and, indeed, hasten the symptoms of old age, even in young persons. As already mentioned, even young girls may acquire some of the attributes of old age by such means. They soon become fat and bloated, the features lose their juvenile aspect, and the cheeks become pendent . . . there is a marked difference between the muscles of a young maiden and those of a woman who has been leading a life of debauchery for some time. The latter will invariably, if not always [*sic*], look older – which ought to be an object lesson. . . .!' The nervous reader is left looking at the words 'too frequent' with apprehension – can he be leading a 'life of debauchery', and will he soon be impotent and have bags under his eyes? What is 'too frequent', anyhow, and is that which is too frequent for me too frequent for you? Recent studies have found people thriving on rates of orgasm which range from a few times a year to ten or twelve times a day – more surprising still, this was known to many observant doctors, and had been for centuries, but the flood of flatulent generalization continued unchecked, and still does.

One gynaecologist writing in a recent B.M.A. publication (or rather republication, since the first edition was withdrawn in deference to organised uproar against an article suggesting that premarital intercourse was common and defensible) mentions that he has often been asked what frequency of intercourse is permitted by law, and whether daily coition is legal! A less inhibited medical writer, Weckerle,[3] who mixed sex with medical gymnastics and recommended the purchase of horizontal bars and a gymnastic mat to enliven matters, was nearer the mark, for all his eccentricities, in opining that 'too much sex never wore out anyone, except a weakling who is out of training' ('*Abgemattet ward durch geschlechtliche Exzesse nur der ungeturnte Weichling*'). But his own recommendations very much overestimate most males' capacity for frequently repeated orgasm. It appears, then, that the first lesson we need to learn in reading almost any literature which purports to advise on, or describe, sexual behaviour (this present book included) is that it is probably for the most part a statement of preference, prejudice and opinion and only a statement of fact where it presents cast-iron evidence based on critical observation.

The traditional view of Christian civilizations has been that all forms of sexual behaviour are by nature suspect, and that only those that make up a bare minimum, essential for the purposes of reproduction, are permissible. This view, from which there has always been a dissenting minority, is being gradually modified in the course of time, and the interpretation of sexual conduct by growing sections of Christian and non-Christian opinion is moving towards the humanist view; but the attitude of the public, of the law, and of many scientific workers remains coloured by the older idea of the inacceptability of sex, even when that idea is rationalized in social terms, or turned inside out to form a doctrine of the supreme importance of sexual experience. In any relationship involving the welfare of others, particularly one that determines the form of the family, and the

17

security of children, strong ethical restraints on conduct are necessary; but such restraints must be based primarily on reasonable grounds, and not upon fear, magic, or unconscious attitudes. They must also come from the individual's own social judgement rather than from external coercion. It is reasonable to say that until such rational and conscious study is possible, and until it is accepted, very little progress is possible on any practical issue.

The dietetic analogy may to some extent serve to explain the need for deliberate study as a basis for sexual ethics to those who argue that, since sexuality is a 'natural' pattern, deliberate attempts to reduce it to rational terms belong to veterinary practice rather than human welfare. Neither the naturalness of a pattern of conduct, nor its occurrence in one or many primitive societies, is very much of a pointer to feasible conduct under conditions of elaborate civilization. Certainly the more wildly unbiological aspects of modern societies must be removed as the price of survival, but even the 'free society' towards which many contemporary politico-social studies are pointing would inevitably involve a complexity of activities and organization that make rational standards essential as a supplement to instinct. It is precisely these standards that have been missing in contemporary urban culture. It may be arguable that neolithic man possessed both a balanced diet and stable sexual relations, although there is no evidence for either of these statements: both dietetics and the scientific study of sexual ethics are required today, because our entire cultural pattern is based upon our need to control our environment and our relationships in rational terms.

At the present time the public turns increasingly to science for the solution of its problems, because it rightly expects that the difficulties individuals and societies encounter in ordering their relationships will prove capable of being tackled by modifications of the method that has brought such eminently successful results in practical issues, such as disease control, and in theoretical problems of ultimate practical interest, such as solar physics. Having the opportunity and the responsibility to remove the whole question of sexual behaviour, which has always proved troublesome to human societies to a greater or lesser degree, from the field of conjecture and myth into the field of observational research, we should be wrong to refuse to intervene in matters of social ethics. But to intervene effectually we need to know:

1. How human beings behave sexually in our own culture, and how this behaviour compares with that of other and former cultures.

2. Which, if any, of the patterns of behaviour are associated with mental abnormality or maladjustment, or have undesirable effects on the participants or on others – the effect of unstable homes upon child development, for example.

3. What pattern of conduct can be upheld with confidence as a general aim – the analogue of a balanced diet in the study of nutrition; variable, as such a diet must be, to suit the circumstances of individuals, not laid down as an ultimate law of conduct.

4. What types of education and social facilities will make the realization of such an optimum pattern possible for most individuals.

A programme of this kind is not in any sense an attempt to organize, canvass, or coerce individuals, or to conduct the relationships of human beings on the lines of a battery hen-house. If we forget the ethical status of sociology, and the fact that individual judgement, even if it is fallible, is the sole basis on which conduct can rest, science will run the risk of making itself as dangerous and as ridiculous as political power has done, and in any case the public will ignore it. The prerequisite of satisfactory relationships of any kind is probably a far greater freedom of personal judgement and initiative than we now possess, but coupled with a supportive social background of community which we still lack, or have progressively lost.

A good deal of present-day insecurity comes from the demands made on the first of these without the backing which individuals would get from the second – they are moderately free, but very much alone. The scientific study of sexuality exists to provide the information upon which the individual, not his would·be guides or rulers, can exercise their judgement. An unparalleled demand for such information exists today among young people of all classes. The social psychologist, if he presents his facts as facts and his opinions as opinions, has discharged his social responsibility as far as it can be discharged; if he attempts to exert pressure other than that of rational argument, he is exceeding his duties.

METHODS OF STUDY

During the Middle Ages, and afterwards throughout the Renaissance, sexual behaviour was studied only to a limited extent, though it received proportionately rather more attention than other biological subjects – the compilers of books of casuistry and of Penitentials appear to have had considerable knowledge of the types of sexual conduct and deviation which they condemned; medicine included the study of infertility and impotence, and prescribed traditional remedies for both; historians and travellers described the customs of other societies, and the Renaissance itself stimulated the study of erotics as a polite accomplishment. The origins of recent work are probably traceable to the renewed interest of Europe in Greek and Roman literature, in which sexuality is freely and integrally discussed, and the classics remained the main source of sexual information for the educated classes until, and after, the end of the eighteenth century.

The early nineteenth-century students of sexual conduct were mostly concerned with compiling information from historical and anthropological sources, but comparatively little of this could be published openly in England. Continental Europe had a larger literature, and it was here that the first studies in sexual psychiatry were made. English knowledge lagged behind: the growth of the middle class had led to the replacement of a culture based on the classics by one based on the Bible, which, unlike much primitive literature, contains little information of a sexual character, and much to relate sexuality to ritual pollution and to sin. It is not long since Acton could describe as a 'foul aspersion' the suggestion that women were capable of orgasm. In this emergent middle class the fear of sexuality and the distrust of its study were extreme, and during the early Industrial period little progress could be made by science in a field so evocative of scandal. The earliest applications of psychology and biology to sexual knowledge coincided with the growth of secularism, very much as the spread of revolutionary liberalism on the Continent has stimulated similar inquiries – Rousseau himself was an unwitting pioneer in this field. Our present knowledge and the toleration of sexual studies in England owe much to the struggle of heretics such as Havelock Ellis and Bradlaugh against the censorship, of Margaret Sanger and others for public sexual education, and to single works of scholarship such as those of Krafft-Ebing, Havelock Ellis, and Sir James Frazer, to say nothing of Burton's *Arabian Nights*, which gave Victorian England its first unexpurgated view of the literature of a non-Christian, non-Hellenistic culture.

To develop a rational approach to sexuality we need information, and accurate information was precisely the factor that was lacking. The first contributions to this body of information came from history and anthropology; they were followed by studies of individual cases of abnormal conduct, and of the case histories of psychopaths and the self-revelations of individuals, by the examination of art and literature, and most recently by means of deliberate statistical surveys. All these approaches are available today, and form the background to the discoveries of psychoanalysis and of comparative sociology. By 1900 most of the patterns of overt sexual behaviour were known, chiefly through the study of cases of sexual deviation. By 1920 Freud had related them to the development of the individual mind. What has been missing, and is still missing, is a clear picture of the relation these patterns bear to the statistical and social norm, and it is this gap the surveys attempt to fill.

Surveys of sexual conduct present special difficulties. Public opposition plays a decreasing part in hindering them; in fact, once they realize that the results will help them with their own doubt and problems the response of most people is enthusiastic,

but special precautions are necessary to avoid highly misleading results – psychopaths tend to volunteer, normal subjects to
censor their answers, statistical random samples require very
elaborate control, and the numerical results are difficult to
interpret. By far the largest, most notorious and most careful
survey so far is that of Kinsey, Pomeroy, and Martin, who
developed a special survey technique to exclude these errors.[42]
Criticism has already been levelled at their results, but there
seems to be no doubt their method will provide useful information. Surveys on a smaller scale, or limited to selected
groups such as students, have provided a certain amount of
factual material but are apt to be misleading. There is already
evidence that patterns of conduct vary widely in various economic strata, even within a single culture, and they manifestly
vary as between nations.[4, 5, 6]

'(The psychiatrist) holds that any obligatory emphasis on any
one mode of sex expression to the exclusion of all others will
usually indicate that some underlying neurotic forces are at
work. . . . . (he) cannot accept any form of sexual activity as inherently and inevitably normal or abnormal. He must always
consider the total setting'.[65]

What is 'normal' cannot be decided by a simple counting of
heads. In medical research of all kinds, normality carries a
double meaning. It may refer to statistical prevalence: in this
case, anxiety states are normal in our society, or hook-worm
infestation in certain parts of America and Africa. For medicine
it also carries an implicit statement of value – normal function
is therefore used to signify optimal function. Some confusion
between these ideas is as inevitable in social science as in older
patterns of morality, unless the two elements are deliberately
isolated. Statistical norms are useful fact-finding mechanisms,
and have value in reassuring those who are preoccupied with
the unusualness of their own conduct. They are not suitable
bases for planning or the setting up of standards, and they certainly carry no suggestion that what is prevalent is desirable.
On the other hand, a demonstration that some practice or
attitude is widespread in otherwise healthy or happy persons
and societies is evidence of its harmlessness, provided that we do

not allow ourselves to be overawed by arguments based upon what is 'natural.'

The type of problem that requires to be solved in assessing 'normality' is very well illustrated by the case of homosexuality. This pattern of behaviour has been traditionally regarded as perverse, later as psychopathic, and certainly as exceptional. The estimate of the percentage of males exhibiting homosexual behaviour has steadily increased, until it has been possible to recognize that, so far from being exceptional, homosexual impulses exist *potentially* in almost all males, and homosexual conduct in a large proportion under suitable circumstances. This in itself suggests to the biologist that the capacity for homosexual response in man, or at least the mechanisms which make him liable to show it, may be evolved adaptations rather than diseases or unfortunate accidents. The idea of homosexuality as a clinical entity or even a 'third sex', which was held by earlier workers, and maintained in self-defence by many writers who recognized such impulses in themselves and required to justify them, is steadily losing ground. In fact, on Freudian grounds, it would appear that the disorder present in the clinical homosexual 'case' is not the presence of homosexual, but the absence of heterosexual, responses. It is only by reference to a statistical norm for a given culture, age group, and social group that concepts of this kind can be gauged. The detailed individual patterns of sexual behaviour in a given culture can also be related to a general human norm – posture in coitus, for instance, which has been regulated to some extent by ideas of what is 'natural', can be shown to vary widely in different societies, and such findings have value in reassuring individual patients: the individual who, in earlier times, might be obsessed by the sinfulness of his impulses may now be obsessed by their abnormality, especially if he can recognize in them the outlines of classificatory concepts such as sadism, masochism, or fetishism.

One exceedingly peculiar feature of human sexuality from the biological standpoint is its instability of object, and the fact that unless the anxiety-loaded phase of development is satisfactorily overcome, there may be partial or complete diversion of sexual interest, especially in the male, away from its normal target to biologically inappropriate objects – a part of the body, an article of clothing, a particular situation, or a member of the same sex, and that these diversions once established have the force of instinct. This is reminiscent of the behaviour of young birds, which pass through a critical phase in which any object presented to them will be recognized as a parent, and followed from then on, with subsequent lack of interest in potential mates which do not resemble it. Most of the grossly atypical responses represent the replacement of the normal drive to mate by some adjacent or substitute object which is, for the normal individual, symbolic or incidental only.

> 'Some symmetry the foot hath with that part
> Which thou dost seek, and is thy map for that
> Lovely enough to stop, but not stay at'

wrote John Donne. The foot-fetishist does stay there, however, to avoid the revival of buried infantile anxiety aroused by going further.

Recognition of the wide range of apparently irrelevant matters to which this sexual 'cathexis' may become attached is one of our chief gains from psychoanalysis in understanding irrational behaviour – thus the recurrent clamour in Britain for the extension or revival of hanging and flogging as punishments is almost certainly due to the fact that these are subjects with a sexual cathexis of this kind (there is never a comparable clamour in favour of other forms of punishment) – in this case there seems to be an added cultural factor, for the same subjects, though sexually symbolic everywhere, seem in other countries to generate less public excitement. Imitative hanging with sexual significance accounts for a few dozen deaths a year, chiefly among adolescent boys – an argument against capital punishment which does not seem to have been put forward very often.

Colour prejudices in an extreme form may also perhaps reflect a different set of cathectic ideas. Oddities of individual behaviour and many forms of crime come under the same heading, and this is not limited to obviously eccentric acts such as

hair-cutting or indecent exposure – stolen property, heterosexual Don Juanism, and fast driving may equally well carry
a compulsive attraction of the same kind.

A particularly interesting feature of the human instability of
sexual object, and of the tendency to sexualize non-sexual
objects, is the constancy with which some topics recur. If
failure to 'imprint' the correct object were the only cause of
these deviations one would expect a fairly wide range of sub-
stitutional preferences – wholly private fetishes do in fact
occur, but there are others which appear so regularly, and in so
many cultures, that they appear to be built in; whether
neurologically or environmentally it would not be wise to
speculate, but this group of reactions may eventually give us
the chance to find out.

Freud points out that such cathexes tend to be 'over-
determined', i.e. to attract for more than one reason – thus
flogging, as a sexual fetish, involves at least four excitant
factors: aggression-domination, movements which simulate
sexual excitement, direct skin stimulation, and reddening of
the buttocks. It is remarkable that this last, which is often
quoted by those who suffer from this obsession as peculiarly
exciting, is a normal sexual releaser in lower primates, which
have 'sex skin' on the posteriors. One can identify a similarly
wide range of factors, biological and psychosymbolic, which
contribute to the popularity of other common fetishes, and
among these there may well be other buried links with our
mammalian past which we still do not recognize.

Similar factors seem to determine the natural history of
individual sexual preferences – there are a few, gross behaviour-
disorders apart, which are of social importance because they lead
to accidents; beside the accidental hangings mentioned above
the pleasure which a few people derive from partial strangula-
tion may easily lead to their own death and a murder charge
against their partner – but the vast majority of human sexual
practices, contrary to a long tradition of medico-religious warn-
ing, are physically harmful only if obviously dangerous or if
they give rise to guilt. They appear to be equally harmless
psychologically, for where they are associated with personality

problems it is the personality problem which generates the un-
usual behaviour not vice versa.

In fact, argument has so involved sexuality with debates
over health and morals that we are apt to miss the fact that
numerically at least the chief biological function of coition in
man is play. In spite of ecclesiastical ideas, the function of
sexual intercourse in man is only comparatively rarely reproductive: it ceased to be predominantly so with the evolution of
the higher primate habit of mating all the year round and
throughout pregnancy, and of constant receptivity in the
female. On the assumption that conception occurs in the 'wild
state' once a year and every year, the maximum proportion of
acts of intercourse which are likely to be 'reproductive' in
function is about 0.5 per cent, and where conception is less
frequent it will be lower. This is a fundamentally different
pattern from that seen, e.g. in the mare, which, like some
devout folk, has intercourse once a year, in foal heat, and only
becomes receptive again if she fails to conceive. Probably the
main function of the frequent coition found in man is social, like
much bird display – it serves primarily to keep the couple
together as a breeding and mutually supporting unit. But it
also seems reasonable to regard sexual intercourse as an important recreation which is biologically very well adapted to
release residual anxieties of all kinds, and which has a physiological means of abreaction – the orgasm – 'built in'. It is, in
other words, the healthiest and most important human sport;
and the need to consider it in other, medical or sociological,
contexts, should never be allowed to obscure the fact.

The balance of evidence suggests that, so far from there
being any firm statistical norm of individual sexual behaviour,
all forms of behaviour exist, or have existed in embryo in every
individual, the differences being differences of emphasis, due to
heredity, environment, early conditioning and the pattern of
the culture in which he lives. Sadism, masochism, fetishism,
homosexuality, and narcissism are all formed by exaggerating
components of a many-stranded sexual impulse, and the pre-
ponderance of these components varies widely in individuals.
A behaviour disorder exists, and requires psychiatric treatment,

only when one of them so far outweighs the others as to cause conflict with society or in the patient's own mind, and usually it then forms part only of a general disturbance of the personality.

It has become important to verify this view especially since enlightened opinion has begun to demand psychotherapy rather than punishment for sex offenders. It is necessary to decide how far the psychiatrist is justified in settling a conflict between an individual and society by upholding an accepted view of 'normality'. Where an isolated homosexual act is committed by by an individual in whom homosexual impulses account only for a small part of his pattern of behaviour, it is hard to determine how far a treatable 'abnormality' can be said to exist. It may be no more than an experiment – though if we say this in court we shall be ensuring, in all probability, a spiteful sentence and a judicial homily on corruption. Judges do not experiment in this field – only in the vicarious satisfactions peculiar to punishment and moralism, which may equally arise from factors in their unconscious development. It is no less important in general psychiatry to know with certainty how far the existence of other atypical patterns of behaviour is to be regarded as abnormal. The hostility of society towards sex has led to an extreme limitation of the forms of sexual behaviour that are generally acceptable: over large sections of Western society, only heterosexual intercourse under restricted conditions of posture and venue is universally regarded as permissible, and other components of the sexual impulse tend to be displaced into non-sexual fields. Most of these other components have a double place in human behaviour – they exist as physiological mechanisms which have acquired secondary psychological overtones. Sadism and masochism are probably, at the physiological level, exaggerations of an instinctive desire for strong skin stimulation and muscular tension during sexual intercourse, but they are also the patterns in which desire to dominate or to be dominated is expressed, and their psychological meaning in man overshadows their original mammalian significance. Homosexuality is possibly a phase in normal development, at least in the male, covering the period at which the desire for sexual activity with another individual co-exists with the association of individuals of one sex – factors that prevent progress from that point, that limit emotional growth, or that restrict opportunity for transference to the other sex may render it permanent.

There is no way of classifying forms of sexual or other behaviour as normal or abnormal *per se* and in a vacuum, on the lines of the ecclesiastic's natural law. If a culture encourages or values a form of sex expression – be it homosexuality or excessive prudery – all those will show it who can; in a culture which discourages it, only those will show it who must. This explains why those sexual emphases which are abnormal in our culture, to the extent that they are compulsive, associated with anxiety, and tend to take up the whole of their proprietor's sexual interest to the detriment of his capacity for normal and unconstrained responses, nearly all turn up in other cultures as accepted sexual techniques: in this case they are learned, and practised not from compulsion but for pleasure or social conformity. The basic psycho-symbolic content and the attraction of such behaviour is the same in each case, but its place in the individual's economy is different. This is true not only of sexual emphases – cannibalism is normal in some cultures, but it is grossly pathological in our own, though it has psycho-symbolic meaning for us, since its symbolism is enshrined in our chief religious rite. But the difference is particularly evident in the different sexual symbols and practices which different cultures cultivate or forbid. Thus homosexual relations between men and boys in classical Greece or Japan, fetishistic interests reflected in the clothing and hair styles of various periods and societies, and a number of practices involving physical aggression, real or token – the flagellomania of some eighteenth- and nineteenth-century English gentlemen, the stylized erotic biting and scratching of Sanskrit, or the erotic bondage of some Chinese and Arabic love manuals, and the (closely related) addiction to tight or deforming clothing, all of which are psycho-symbolically significant – the insistence of various societies on adopting or avoiding particular coital postures, the extensive orogenital play in others, all occur sporadically in our own culture. When they do so it is usually through an inner compulsion sufficient to override custom, and they are quite commonly seen in disturbed people who ask to be relieved of them by psycho-analysis. Culturally inculcated emphases, such as the typical anti-sexuality of Western Christendom, are not recognized as deviations, though their roots are equally in psychopathology, and they would astonish other cultures as much as a cannibal or a corset fetishist astonishes us. The significance of any form of sexual interest, then, depends on the place it occupies in the individual's economy, while the whole range of common potential emphases are the ingredients of our sexual behaviour as a species. One effect of widening knowledge, particularly knowledge of comparative anthropology, appears to be a widening of the spectrum of overt behaviour which is culturally accepted, and a lessening of anxiety in those who have a com-pulsion towards such atypical behaviour – the steady weaken-ing of the long-standing taboo against orogenital contact in Anglo-American society which was once a cause of great guilt and marital strife, is a case in point; we now recognize such con-tact as normal, unless it swamps all other sexual activities and becomes an obsession, and for this lessening of anxiety, biological and psychological reassurance is probably directly responsible.

We can equally easily make false generalizations about the psychological 'meaning' of behaviour in other cultures. Societies which tolerated homosexuality or promiscuity have long been denounced by moralists as 'degenerate' – regardless of the fact that there have been societies in which refusal to eat one's mother instead of burying her would be good evidence of a disturbed state of mind. An Englishman who burned incense grains on his mistress's abdomen and stuck needles into her by way of sexual excitation would be very likely to be a patho-logical sadist – a medieval Chinese who did the same would only be using an accepted and respectable form of physio-therapy which is still popular in Chinese medicine as a tonic, though in fact the unconscious significance of the actions, as well as the physical discomfort they produced, might well be the same in both cases.

Forms of behaviour, then, have to be considered in the light of what is known of their unconscious origin, in the light of what is customary or tolerated in a given culture, and in the light of the part they play in the individual's mental economy – of who does what, and when and where. It is disproportionate, if we are interested in *social* effects, to lay much emphasis on the kind of physical variation or deviation in behaviour which I have been discussing – such object deviations are of great biological and psychoanalytical interest, because of the light they may throw on the way in which human sexual 'releasers' operate, but by far the most important social deviations are those which affect the general maturity of sexual behaviour, ability to behave responsibly, and capacity for stable emotional relationships. These are far less clearcut, and much less is known about them, but their social importance is very great, because they profoundly affect the pattern of home life and are likely in turn to affect the personalities of the children. It is an unfortunate consequence of the pattern of sexual interest in man that these unsensational forms of immaturity lack the cathectic content which focuses attention on peculiarities of *physical* behaviour and makes the study of them attractive.

In general, too, the directly sexual expression of such deviations has less social importance than their appearance in non-sexual fields. Sadism and masochism are widespread elements in our make-up – a study of modern films and cartoon strips indicates their efficacy as erotic symbols; in sexual relations, minor manifestations of this kind may not be socially important, provided they are chiefly symbolic and nobody is actually hurt. When such impulses spill over into non-sexual fields, however, they may do much harm both to the individual and to the community. Narrow conceptions of normality have done much to insure such a spillover; abnormal emphases are increased by lack of outlet, and the possibility of working out aberrant fantasies in a harmless form within the structure of sexual behaviour is very much limited. The man who dares not admit to his wife that he has a desire to beat her, or at least pretend to do so, may express his disappointment in the advocacy of bigger and better floggings for criminals; the man who dares not express the sexual significance which he finds in female undergarments may become a clamourer against 'obscene' Underground posters, or find himself involved in charges of indecent assault (sometimes both). Of the common deviations, only sadism and masochism, because of their effects on non-sexual attitudes and their association with aggression and injury, are of any lasting social importance. 'Except in borderline states sadomasochistic fantasies are usually playful. The patients would be repelled by the opportunity to act them out: when the fantasy includes a partner, both are represented as knowing that the activity is playful.'[68] People who behave like Jack the Ripper are fortunately few, and can be segregated – delegates to Party Congresses who howl their approval of hanging and flogging are by contrast numerous, and can be neither segregated nor shamed.

It is obviously impossible for science to give accurate information on the significance of individual behaviour, either to the public or to bodies such as courts of law, until it has the information to give. As long as the assessment of statistical normality depended on guesswork, on convention, and on the examination of the life stories of those who were driven to the doctor by their sexual and mental problems, no such information was forthcoming. The work of the future will be based on studies of comparative institutions and behaviour, similar to those carried out by Malinowski and Mead among primitive folk, and on the application of anthropological methods to our own society, the study of a community in some respects more savage, though technically more advanced, than any of those which provided the classical material of anthropology. The science of human society and behaviour is more and more adopting the same observational methods and statistical analysis that have brought results in the study of animal behaviour. Human zoology of this kind does not exclude the forming of judgements of values: it is the material upon which judgements of values and of ethics can stand, because, from such a basis, they can be reached without prejudging any of the issues that affect us emotionally.

Our generation has seen this ideal of sensible enjoyment

brought within reach, and it is an objective well worth pursuing. In this book I will try to indicate the type of problems that are to be solved, and the type of help in solving them that we can expect from social science. My detailed conclusions are a matter of opinion, to be revised by subsequent knowledge wherever they are the result of my own prejudice unsupported by data; but the method and standpoint of social science in the study of sexual behaviour have become sufficiently definite to be presented with confidence, and their importance is likely to grow.

II

The Biological Background [6, 10, 60]

THE separate branches of science have the opportunity of choosing how they propose to treat their material; when the material is man and his behaviour, the choice is an extraordinarily wide one. How far older cultures, for whom sexuality was a less alarming and emotive subject than it is in our own, could form any idea of the general pattern of human sexual behaviour it is hard to say. They were certainly more familiar with its manifestations in everday life. But our own civilization is certainly the first which has had the equipment to make such a study in scientific terms, by the observational methods that have produced results in other fields, and to form estimates of the significance of the various patterns.

An initial picture of man the animal must precede any study of man the individual or man the social unit. In a subject where many fields of study join, it is useful to work through contrasting, supplementary approaches. Biology and zoology made an earlier start than psychology – sociology is relatively a newcomer. The amount of solid fact each can contribute is roughly proportional to the time for which it has existed as an independent study. From the biological standpoint, human sexual physiology is fairly well known; we cannot yet give as clear a picture of the pattern of sexual behaviour in man as we can for many birds and mammals, but we know considerably more about its development and significance.

The sexual behaviour of animals other than man is typically instinctive. It tends to be stereotyped, and it occupies only a limited place in the general pattern of behaviour, since it is evoked directly by hormonal changes, and follows, as a rule, a limited cyclical pattern. Human beings show some instinctive behaviour, and this behaviour is determined in the same way, but the far greater importance of higher mental functions in man makes it more difficult to identify. The cyclical pattern is also far less marked. Many female mammals display sexual behaviour only at infrequent intervals, when they are actually capable of being impregnated by the male: the continuous monthly cycle in the human female is accompanied by variations in sexual desire, but these are not very consistent, and mating, though not necessarily conception, can take place at any stage in the cycle. Seasonal and cyclical mating in man are usually features of primitive rather than civilized cultures: in evolution, the change to continuous mating occurs between lower and higher primates. The main landmark in the development of reproductive behaviour is therefore not the period of 'heat', occurring at longish intervals, and alternating with stretches of time in which mating behaviour is absent, but puberty, the onset of full reproductive capacity.

Puberty in both sexes is hormonally determined, though the mechanism which times its onset is not fully understood. Its timing is under genetic control, since early and late puberty both run in families. The 'clock' mechanism appears to be situated in the hypothalamus of the brain. Puberty is more gradual in man than in most animals, lasting over a period of years, and it is conveniently dated in the female from the first menstrual period, although changes in body contour and awakening of adult instinctive patterns may occur earlier. In the male, it is less possible to fix an arbitrary date, the growth of beard and pubic hair, the change in voice, and the onset of adolescent masturbation being spread over a period of time. Adolescence coincides with important psychological changes, and with the emergence of the adult level of intelligence, but the two are not causally related, since either may appear first. The time of onset shows considerable racial and individual variation. Over most of Western Europe, the age of puberty in both boys and girls has come down by about five years over the last century with a corresponding acceleration in other indices of development. This may well represent a return to normal, however, after a period in which puberty was delayed by adverse social factors: the mean age of first menstruation in English girls is roughly that which seems to have obtained in Roman and medieval times. There are also large differences in developmental rate between individuals. These are related to the general shape and build of the body – they have a special importance which we shall encounter later in this chapter.

So long as sexuality and mating behaviour were regarded as identical, all sexual manifestations in normal subjects were believed to begin at puberty. In birds and animals, especially primates, primitive sexual behaviour may occur even in infancy.[60] But human sexuality, because of its non-reproductive functions, has other roots which are in existence long before reproduction is possible. We owe the idea of this double pattern of sexuality to Freud,* and evidence in support of his original work has accumulated steadily since his time. Freud showed that the changes that take place at puberty represent not an emergence of a new impulse, which has been latent before that, but the expression in specifically reproductive behaviour of impulses that have been present since birth. It is justifiable to regard all these impulses, from birth to puberty, as well as after puberty, as a continuous pattern, and the ultimate reproductive expression of the underlying drive can be profoundly modified in form by influences during childhood. The expression of these impulses before puberty takes forms appropriate to age and physical development, but these component, partial forms of expression participate in the fully developed pattern of mating behaviour, and accidental causes in infancy and childhood can make any one of them predominate, even to the exclusion of normal reproduction.

In a simplified form, this whole body of impulse can be regarded as an undifferentiated desire for physical and emotional pleasure. Its aim at any age will depend upon the stage of development that has been reached, and we can interpret these stages in terms of physiology. The newborn infant experiences pleasure chiefly through sucking; at a later stage, interest shifts to the control of bowel function and urination,

*Freud's work is best summarized in his own lectures. No subsequent exposition of them is livelier or more intelligible. (7)

functions that have an anatomical and evolutionary association with the reproductive organs; later, at the age of four or five, there is a commencing shift of interest to the genital organs. There are, of course, other factors in this pattern of gratification, and its development now appears to be less tidy than Freud thought, but the progress is recognizably similar in all human infants. During these early phases the child's pursuit of satisfaction (*libido*) is limited to the experiences of his own body, and this whole phase was termed by Freud the 'autoerotic'. Its chief importance lies in the fact that during these first four stages the results which follow the child's experimental attempts to find satisfaction exert a profound effect on his whole personality. If these are halted at any stage, anxieties drawn from that or an earlier stage are likely to colour his subsequent behaviour both in sexual and non-sexual fields.

Freud had found that conscious behaviour, normal and abnormal, in his adult patients was influenced by thought-patterns which were unconscious and followed non-rational lines; much of the content of these was sexual, and appeared to date from early childhood, and there was an extremely powerful block to making the unconscious significance of this imagery conscious. The imagery itself showed a striking preoccupation with three topics – the external genitals, fantasies of incest, and fears of castration.

This system of unconscious imagery and associated anxieties Freud called the Oedipus complex, after the Greek hero who killed his father, inadvertently married his mother, and blinded (or castrated) himself in expiation. It appeared to date from one particular period of childhood between the ages of four and six, and a constant ingredient in it was intense anxiety over the anatomical differences between the sexes, linked, in the male, with an extraordinary fear of injury to his own genitalia. The whole outburst of anxiety appeared to be connected with another mechanism Freud has been obliged to postulate – the sexual attraction of the male child to its mother, and its resentment or fear of the father as a rival who was at once loved and hated. In both sexes the female genitalia were a focus of this anxiety, the male child seeing them as a wound and a castration threat, the female child believing herself to be in fact 'short of something'.

Freud was initially as impressed as we must be by the oddity of this. At first he put it down to injudicious threats by parents to 'cut off' the penis of the child who masturbated, but it soon became clear that the fear arose independently of threats. Once this particular irrational train of thought was recognized, echoes of it could be seen all over human behaviour, in places where the psychoanalyst could not possibly have put it.

To a modern biologist the story seems far less implausible than it did when Freud discovered it.[60] In the first place, the Oedipal responses, which have every appearance of being built in, look very like a temporary mental organ with a function – 'The Oedipus complex is not normal in the way that the nose is normal: rather it is like the thymus gland – it is normal at a certain period but abnormal if it persists beyond that period. Everybody has it between the ages of four and six – later in normal people it seems to vanish'[8]. The Oedipal situation, moreover, not only explains a vast amount of otherwise inexplicable human behaviour – it has come to fit progressively better and better into what we know of the course of human evolution and of animal behaviour generally.

Sexuality in its usual sense implies reproduction. The idea of infantile sexuality, and the presence of elaborate sexual impulses far ahead of reproductive maturity, as Freud described them, would be an instance of what is called 'anticipation' – the shifting of an adult mental or physical structure into early life. The Oedipal reactions with their peculiar genital content are obviously likely to be connected with this shift. The castration fear, in particular, has every appearance of being – though Freud, because of his own terminology, would not use the term – instinctive. Such a fear, as Freud thought, might be connected with competition between father and son – but how and why?

To offer a possible answer we need to look at two biological ideas which, though known, were not emphasized in Freud's time. The first is the fact that human childhood differs from that of all other mammals in the shape of its developmental curve. The development which in lower animals is continuous is interrupted in man by a long lag-period inserted between the fifth and the ninth year, which cuts it into two – an early phase, which is separated from sexual maturity by the whole length of childhood, and a pre-reproductive phase which coincides with puberty and the appearance of the secondary sex characters. The two peaks of psychosexual development and the intervening latency period which Freud postulated therefore fit accurately over two periods of somatic growth, separated by a latent period.

The second fact is the recognition that in most family-breeding animals, special mechanisms are necessary to prevent competition between adults and their own children. In general, the existence of a long-term, pair-mating family situation involves two requirements: that other sexually active individuals should be driven away (usually by the male, who defends his 'territory') and that the accepted mate should not. Various behavioural and visual 'releaser' mechanisms exist in birds to achieve this. The other permitted intruders on the territory are, of course, the young – these are usually protected by the fact that they do not become sexually competitive until they develop the characteristic plumage, song, etc. of the adult – the secondary sexual characters.

It has long been obvious that castration anxiety, which seems quite out of place in the context of human societies, but appears as if it ought to have a function, would be much less inappropriate if it occurred in an animal with no latent period. It could then serve to make the young male avoid his father over the critical period between becoming recognizably male and becoming fully adult. On this scale it would still occur well ahead of the secondary sex characters, which would appear in man, if there were no latent period, about the age of nine. But psycho-analytical experience has made it quite clear that this anxiety is in some way triggered by the genitalia themselves. This may well be an important clue to its origin. Both the timing and the content of the Oedipal anxieties in man would be intelligible if they evolved in pair-mating animals, where dependence on the mother was long and getting longer, and where for some reason *the genitalia themselves had suddenly come to replace the secondary sex characters as sexual recognition signals,* so that males were competitive almost as soon as they could walk, and long before they were mature. This could well be a by-product of quite unrelated changes – loss of hair, erect posture, or even growing intelligence, which associated male organs with male sex characters and responded to them by automatic aggression. This would call for a major adaptation in behaviour. If male children must love their mother, in order to stay in the family, but avoid her during sexual activity in order not to be treated as intruders, avoidance of the displaying female as a 'castration threat', and ambivalence towards the father, in which his genitalia served as a dominance signal, would fill this function admirably.

This is a speculative explanation, but one which accommodates most of the peculiarities of the Oedipal reactions. One would naturally try to confirm it by looking for similar behaviour in other primates, but it has to be remembered that there are no living primate *ancestors* of man, and the modern apes may differ from him precisely in having failed to evolve it. It has been suggested that in modern apes, the 'Oedipal' situation is never outgrown, but remains as a lifelong balance between the desire to mate and the need to defer to larger males.[9] Among apes, too, it is said that an unsuccessful battle with a larger male may in fact produce not physical but functional castration by interfering with the loser's potency – this seems to be the situation which the human Oedipal fears were 'designed' to avoid.[10]

In any event, the existence of these reactions makes it necessary in man for the sexual impulse to undergo reversal and re-shaping in a unique way, and any miscarriage of the process which causes the Oedipal avoidance of the female to persist will affect the pattern of adult behaviour. The persistence of this peculiar pattern in spite of functional ambiguities and long after the need which produced it suggests that it has acquired a fresh function; this appears to be the shaping of adult character structure. One consequence of the need to 'forget' the Oedipal phase is the phenomenon of repression, and the sharp division of the human mind into conscious and un-conconscious parts: it is this rather than intelligence alone which underlies both the human capacity for conceptual thought, and the fact that residues from these irrelevant child-hood patterns, if repressed in fact, can continue to influence adult behaviour unawares.

If this explanation is correct, even in the most general way, it more than accounts for the uniqueness of sex as a topic of human concern. The existence of the Oedipal fears, and the un-certainty of the process of outgrowing them expose man to the risk of imperfect character-development (neurosis) particularly in fields affecting his sexual behaviour. Freud offered no ex-planation of the reason why some people lose their childhood responses normally while others do not. Failure is usually put down to psychological trauma in childhood: the variation in individual developmental rates in man and the shape of the human growth curve also, raise the possibility – wholly specula-tive at the moment[11, 12] – that genetic or environmental factors affecting developmental rate might play a part, in view of the large part which rate changes have already played in the evolution of human childhood behaviour. It is evident from the curve that since the Oedipal reactions occur close to an in-flection, a small differential change in rates of behavioural development might shift them bodily like the bubble in a spirit level along the 'plateau' of delayed growth, and make the difference between their persistence all through the formative period and their disappearance at the proper time. More detailed evidence to show why some of us react to infant ex-periences by adult disturbance, and others not, has yet to be sought. Separation from the mother through a childhood illness has been found in the histories of some fetishistic subjects [54, 55] – the operative factor here could be either physical or psychological. In an epileptic subject a fetish has been excised by a brain operation[63]. In all, the settling of the sex object in man is a complex business. It is interesting that among birds some burrowing species, which do not see their parents at the nesting age, owing to the darkness of the burrow, seem to have similar trouble in imprinting the correct sex object, and have compensated by evolving extra-brilliant plumage (wood duck, kingfisher).[58, 59] This is a matter for future students of the physical causes of psychological misdevelopment and the genetics of neurosis to examine. I mention it here, and I have discussed the work of Freud at some length in *biological* rather than psychological terms, to indicate how well it fits into the general pattern of biological thinking. So far from being biologically disreputable, Freud's mode of approaching human behaviour, even where he was probably mistaken, has been increasingly in line with the rest of biological thought.[13]

The earliest physical manifestations of sexuality in action are such phenomena as suckling, or the interest of a baby in its excreta. The next phases, since they concern the genital organs, have always been recognized as sexual and have been regarded unfavourably by societies such as our own. Manipulation of the genitals may appear early in infancy, though it is most common after the end of the early autoerotic period. The mechanism of genital stimulation exists very early; erection may be observed in very young babies but is purely reflex at this age. The infantile form of masturbation is closely comparable to other childhood habits, such as thumb-sucking, and has, of course, no reproductive content. The onset of puberty in the male is generally accompanied by a renewal of masturbation, which leads to orgasm, the intervening years being occupied with the child's awakening interest in other children and by his desire to see and touch their bodies and to exhibit his own. Masturbation of the adolescent type is almost universal in civilized societies, but the fact that it is discovered accidentally or learned from other children suggests that it is not strictly instinctive in man. In social groups that permit sexual intercourse at a very early age, it may not appear at all,[14] in fact, there may be no real 'latent period' in a social sense, child play merging with adolescent courtship.[15] The tendency in civilized societies is for masturbation to act as a substitute for coitus until marriage is socially or economically permitted. During the period in which it predominates, sexual play with members of the same sex is probably rather commoner than with members of the opposite sex – this again is largely determined by customs and institutions, though there is some evidence that homosexual play of this kind has a function in the development of sexuality. In almost all societies that impose restrictions on sexual intercourse the earliest heterosexual attempts are of the nature of equivalents, and in our own society 'petting', in the sense of sexual play short of coitus, represents an intermediate stage.

The 'gender role' which an individual adopts – 'manly' or "womanly" – according to the standards of his culture, is oddly enough almost wholly learned, and little if at all built in; in fact, the gender role learned by the age of two years is for most individuals almost irreversible, even if it runs counter to the physical sex of the subject. The gender role appears to be acquired by a complicated process of unconscious imitation and acquisition from both parents – hence the tendency for all of us to harbour some attributes normally referred to the other sex, which may become manifest in special situations, or remain as a shadowy second-self, Jung's *animus* and *anima*, man-in-woman and woman-in-man. Different societies differ considerably in what they expect their men and women to be, and one society may set different standards at different times. Beards are alternately manly and effeminate, women may be expected to faint away or to drive tractors and land with airborne troops, dress may be as ornate in either sex, or as plain, as the diversity of plumage in the sexual dimorphism of birds. At the moment, it is a reasonable generalisation that the role of the sexes is getting more alike than it was in the immediate past – so far as rights, demands, activities and behaviour are concerned. It might be asked if this sex equality is likely to confuse or blur sex-object fixation and gender role in our children – some have thought that it may. But the differences between the roles assigned to man and woman have not been abolished, only made subtler, and the child of 'imprinting' age seems to have faculties specially attuned to this kind of discrimination.

Human mating behaviour, as we have seen, can contain elements that are derived from very nearly all the infantile forms of expression. It is also heavily influenced by residual anxieties of various kinds which reflect those of the childhood phase. The extent of this range of variation in other cultures has been obscured for our own society by the extremely small numbers of these component parts which we look upon as acceptable. Patterns of conduct outside this range have for centuries been regarded, both by science and by the public, as abnormal. The *mores* of our society, in their stricter form, used to restrict the expressions of sexuality within adult marriage to mouth-to-mouth kisses, and to coitus in one position, which most commonly takes place in darkness. Other cultures have not limited themselves in this way. The range of typical heterosexual behaviour in human beings includes oral and manual stimulation of the mouth and lips, the erogenous zones of the skin, the breasts, and the genitals. It also includes the whole range of custom relating to clothes, decoration of the body with paint and jewellery, which are modified by climate; variation in coital posture, which tends to become stereotyped within a culture, as in our own; and a number of other practices which spring from one or another of the primitive sexual impulses. The extent to which such a variation has been developed depends largely on the attitude a culture has adopted toward sexuality in general. Stable civilizations that developed privacy and leisure for sections of their population have tended to develop the range of sexual practice as a social asset and have produced a considerable erotic literature. In these cultures, mating behaviour underwent very much the same social transformation as cookery or dancing and was converted into a source of pleasure and recreation independent of its primary function. Western European cultures between the end of the Roman Empire and the present day have developed predominantly in the opposite direction. They have come to repudiate all cultural elaboration of physical sexuality and to prohibit most of its manifestations, either by law or by a deep-seated public distaste. This repudiation has extended to the exhibition of the naked body, to many forms of coitus, to oral stimulation other than the mouth-to-mouth kiss, to atypical but historically widespread activities such as homosexuality, and even to heterosexual coitus itself, which has been regarded as a compromise with an ideal standard of virginity. While most cultures have restricted one or another of the manifestations of sexuality, our own has gradually come to reject all of them, and to erect institutions making no allowance for their expression. This raises an important biological issue. So long as institutions such as schools or prisons are run on the assumption that sexual expression is unnecessary, at least before adult marriage, and the individual, in attempting to conform to the *mores* of his society, is obliged to accept long periods, or a lifetime, of sexual abstinence, it becomes important for us to know how far such abstinence is, in fact possible, and what its effects are upon health.

When this question is put to the sexual psychologist in general terms, he is bound to be aware that his answer will be taken to uphold or demolish an entire ethical system, and he may very well be influenced accordingly. The remarks of Freud on sublimation have been adopted by many writers as a simple answer to an awkward problem, and an increasing number of people who no longer accept the religious dogma on which the advocacy of abstinence was based have attempted to live in conformity with the custom of their society by the sublimation of their sexual desires. A large number of popular works contain categorical statements that 'continence is not harmful', but usually draw no distinction between abstinence from pre-marital coitus and abstinence from all forms of sexual activity, which must be vanishingly rare. The true answer cannot be given categorically, but a great deal of factual information is accumulating from the study of individual behaviour. This suggests that the capacity for abstinence and the resistance to sexual deprivation vary widely in individuals. The normal frequency of sexual intercourse covers such a wide range that questions of the possibility of abstinence can be answered only for a known individual; it has been stated[14] that the most prominent instances of total sexual abstinence without ill effect are in reality instances of an innately low sexual vitality. Individual needs certainly vary here as in every other human context. What can be said with confidence is that examples of complete abstinence for long periods of time are extremely rare, the place of normal coitus in such individuals being taken by other sexual outlets such as masturbation. The evidence in most animals,* even those which exhibit only infrequent sexual activity, is that the effects of chronic *enforced* abstinence are harmful and tend to result in manifestations closely similar to human anxiety. No definite evidence is available to prove that sublimation can account in most people for more than a part of the total sexual drive, and its results are not in general demonstrably desirable. Kinsey[14] summarizes the results of his statistical findings as follows:

> A great many persons have tried to establish their sexual lives on the assumption that sublimation is possible, and the outcome desirable. . . . Fundamentally apathetic persons are the ones who are most often moral (conforming to the *mores*), most insistent that it is a simple matter to control sexual response, and most likely to offer themselves as examples of the possibility of the diversion of probably non-existent sexual energies. But such inactivity is no more sublimation . . . than blindness, deafness or other perceptive defects. If . . . one removes those who are physically incapacitated, natively low in sexual desire, sexually unawakened in their younger years, separated from their usual sources of stimulation, or timid and upset by their repressions, there are simply no cases which remain as clear-cut examples of sublimation.

It seems clear that while some transference of 'sexual energy' to other fields may occur, a complete repudiation of sexual activity is almost as unlikely in practice as a complete repudiation of food, and that the products of such a repudiation are more likely to be pathological than constructive. Its main result is to produce feelings of guilt and shame in regard to sexual activity, rather than to prevent it.

* It has been shown that in rats regular mating leads to greater longevity and increases resistance to chemical and biological poisons, infection, and stress. In some animals, therefore, it seems that regular sexual intercourse is necessary for the optimal functioning of the endocrine system. There is no direct evidence that this occurs in man, although several pelvic conditions in women may perhaps be related to failure to bear children. The greater longevity of married people is probably the result of other factors. (Agduhr, E., and Barron, D. H. (1938), *Arch. Int. Pharmacodynam. et Therap.* 58, 351: Agduhr, E. (1939), *Acta Medica Scand.*, 99, 387.)

Sex in Society

If this is the case, we have to ask ourselves how it is that an attitude of repudiation which is not, at root, feasible in its implications ever came into existence. Several pointers to the answer are available. The first is that modern Western societies are not morally homogeneous. The conduct which is acceptable at various educational levels is in some cases so diverse that the levels behave sexually as different societies. Kinsey has produced statistics to show that a distribution of this kind exists in the United States at the present time. Extramarital intercourse is most widely accepted in the lower educational groups, masturbation and 'petting' in the higher. Similar differences exist in the acceptance of patterns of mating behaviour – coital posture, nakedness, oral stimulation of the genital organs, and the admission of homosexual relationships. The *mores* of the groups differ, but in no single group do they coincide with the moral outlook of the law or of corporate society. Confirmation of this view is needed, and it is not clear how far a similar distribution exists in England. It does, however, fit a number of the observed facts. The peculiar position of the law and of authority in relation to this system of standards gives us another clue. The law might be expected to reflect at least the *mores* of the ruling class, but this is not the case. What it does very often reflect is the influence of the most disturbed and prohibitive section of the community.

Kinsey[14] compared the moral attitude of a known group of individuals with their mean frequencies of sexual outlet and noted that the demands made by each for the exercise of restriction and of abstinence by others, and by society, were almost exactly in inverse proportion to their own sexual requirements.

The mystic and occult philosopher Ouspensky[16] observed that institutional morals owe their origin not to the ruling class as a whole but to the least sexually active section of it, the 'infra-sex', who tended to compensate for their animal deficiencies by developing an abnormally strong desire to regulate the conduct of others. This theory has support from the study of sexual abnormality, though repression rather than animal deficiency is probably the chief factor in the matter.

46

The Biological Background

The example of the American purity-crusader Comstock is an extreme case: this individual devoted most of his life to the detection of supposedly obscene literature, an activity that assumed, for him, the proportions of a sexual substitute. In the wider sense, it is generally admitted that frustration or extreme feelings of guilt in sexual matters may lead to the development of a particular form of aggressive conduct that manifests itself in the desire for unlimited authority. There is a growing suggestion in the available evidence that while membership of a ruling class depends upon economic circumstance, the desire to govern, especially in highly centralized communities, is not infrequently a manifestation of this type of aggression.

This speculation raises issues too wide to pursue here – but it seems to be true that prohibitors aim to be legislators, while non-prohibitors are more inclined to mind their own business – hence the tendency of institutions to reflect the least liberal view of sex.

III

The Social Background and Its Problems

THE PATTERN OF ASOCIAL SOCIETIES

A NY attempt to isolate sexual behaviour from the other factors in a social pattern is bound to hinder our comprehension of it and to lead to false emphases. Societies are the direct products of their economic, historical, and climatic background, and, as such, they require to be studied as wholes. Modern urban societies have certainly more than their share of sexual problems when we compare them with some simpler patterns of life, but these problems in our own time form an integral part of a larger problem of personal insecurity, endemic anxiety, and the breakdown of fundamental social adjustments. On the other hand, they are free from other distresses – death of infants and children, death in childbirth, and many diseases which have always, until now, been a part of the human scene.

It is not yet possible to say with accuracy whether sexual frustration is predominantly a cause or an effect of these contemporary problems: it can be shown to operate both as cause and as effect, and an increase in sexual maladjustment was part of a growing tendency away from workable patterns of living that has been manifest in industrial civilizations since the middle of the nineteenth century. Now there are signs that it is beginning to remedy itself, but the new societies are characterized by a mixture of prosperity and isolation which many people are clearly finding it difficult to handle. The state of these modern urban civilizations has been called asociality, and this is as good a sociological term of abuse as any. Their underlying pattern, allowing for the differences of circumstance which

48

exist between countries, shows a number of common features. Before the Industrial Revolution, English society passed through a series of relatively stable phases, which involved progressive but slow change in patterns of government, agriculture, industry, and belief. The pace of these changes, and their effects on individual life, never for long succeeded in outstripping the power of the individual to adjust himself to them. In the hundred and fifty years following the Industrial Revolution, the entire pattern has been rapidly modified. The effect of industrialization was to produce an enormous growth of the urban population, much of which consisted of a proletariat living under slum conditions and separated within one generation from modes of living and thought which had been little modified in centuries, and from their traditional system of behaviour. The forming of large industrial cities at the expense of self-contained small groups was followed by the superficially stable period of Victorianism, but the disruption spread very rapidly below this surface, and the equilibrium reached by the new industrial society was shortlived.

The problems we are facing today are the long-term consequences of this series of changes and of its effects on individual life. The centralized life of post-industrial Western civilizations has certain characteristic features, which are ominously like those that preceded the collapse of older societies. A striking increase in the material amenities, and the complexity, of living, and in the range of activities possible for the individual, has been offset by an equally striking concentration of the power of decision in the hands of professional governments, democratic as well as tyrannical, and a corresponding reduction in the actual field of individual activity. We are often dealing with a society in which the family is the largest coherent social unit, a family whose members tend to drop off at puberty, and whose survival time is limited to one, or at most two, generations; in which the chief cultural focus is urban, and a large part of the urban population does not know the name of its next-door neighbour but two; in which human activities are increasingly limited to techniques, and the techniques to groups actively engaged in earning a living by them; in which the inflation of

49

authority has virtually abolished coherent patterns of individual responsibility, and in which very nearly all the older activities that made up the background of human conduct and behaviour have been delegated to central authority – congested but lonely, technically advanced but personally insecure, subject to a complicated mechanism of institutional order but individually irresponsible and confused for lack of communal sanction. The central features of such a society are chronic but kick-hunting boredom, an immense inflation of the real power of the administration, and a steady loss by the individual of control over his personal relationships and of his sense of position in a social group.

The sexual problems of a society of this kind are largely manifestations of anxiety – some of it endogenous, and coming from our own personal makeup, some of it generated by our fellows. The outlets for aggressive behaviour, itself not abnormal, which exist in social societies, have been largely removed. Such impulses, deprived of possible constructive value, can provide a reservoir of fear, anxiety, and irrational attitudes in the public at large; the professional concentration of politics, and the increase in the size of the units the state controls with ease and speed, greatly aggravate the strain which rests on the ruling group and the extent of the damage which their prejudices and misjudgements can produce. This combination of factors increases the tendency for psychopaths to achieve power, and for those in power to become psychopathic. It tends to involve reasonably sane administrators in policies as glaringly schizophrenic as the atomic arms race, the 'doomsday machine' or the extermination camps – by easy stages, as it were. A succession of economic booms and slumps, with their political consequences, and of a growing militarism linked to a growing vulnerability over the last two generations has heightened the atmosphere of anxiety and disorientation.

Even so, the consequences of change are not wholly bad – they rarely are. The contrast between the end-product and the Britain of 1901 is between a society in which all but a liberal minority set out with enthusiasm to 'flatten Kruger', and a society in which the political leadership is glumly but rigidly committed to a 'deterrent' which may end history, the adult public is largely numb, and the younger generation demonstrates devotedly against nuclear weapons, or fights among itself out of sheer frustration.

The older sociology regarded institutions as the means by which individual behaviour is moulded and controlled. The entire emphasis of the asocial society, in its attempts to control individual conduct and the manifestations of individual aggression, is still institutional. Both governments and revolutionary movements tend to look upon institutions as means of salvation, to be upheld or altered. But older patterns of law rested ultimately on the traditional standards (*mores*) of the group, and from the observation of a society like our own, in which institutions exist increasingly in isolation, we can say with certainty that the part such institutions play in determining conduct is extremely limited. This is particularly obvious in sexual behaviour, where the *mores* of individual strata of society bear little relationship to laws and are almost uninfluenced by them. But with the confusion and destruction of older *mores* and patterns of belief, the attempts at institutional control tend to become more and more frenzied, and the symptomatic changes in sexual attitude are treated as root causes of the entire pattern of collapse. The emotional content of sex may increase the ease with which the discontents of the public and the ruling groups are vented against sexually abnormal individuals and against the pursuit of sexual studies in general; or unorthodox sexual behaviour may itself acquire the tone of a general protest against 'things like they are'.

Even the emphasis on sexual conflict which has provided the groundwork of psychoanalysis is possibly itself a socially conditioned emphasis, at least to the extent that society now gives virtually no support to the problem-bearing individual. He is increasingly 'free to choose', but painfully solitary.

Sexual normality in asocial societies is attacked and hindered at more than one level. All stable personal relationships demand a basic minimum of security, and the effects of chronic anxiety and disorientation on the individual temper are sufficient to explain part at least of the large body of unsuccessful marriages. At the physiological level, anxiety is as much a hindrance to sexual as to digestive function. The institutionalism of modern societies knows only one incentive and one deterrent: fear. Fear is employed as a means of influencing behaviour at every level, from patent-medicine advertising based on 'body odour' to 'blood, sweat, and tears'. Compared with politicians, advertizers now more commonly combine it with hope, but it is a long time since any positive hope won an English election. And while fear continues to be a prominent cohesive force and a predominant means of government, the modern individual, separated from the support of sociality, is subject at once to perpetual indoctrination with it, to a large number of rapidly moving dangers inherent in the use of machinery and mechanical transport, and to a new social insecurity. Animals tend to live at interchangeable levels of attention; alarm behaviour is a response to hostile environment, which lasts only so long as the need for sudden action exists and which involves a suspension of many 'vegetative' functions such as digestion and reproduction. The modern man frequently lives under circumstances which evoke this alarm behaviour in a chronic form. He is compelled to maintain a preparedness for 'fight or flight', which leads to definite physiological effects. A society that exhibits perpetual sympathotonia might be predicted, experimentally, to be dyspeptic, constipated, and impotent, and almost any column of advertisements lends colour to such a view. Some manifestations at least of sexual dysfunction probably belong to the growing group of psychosomatic diseases, which includes peptic ulcer, hypertension, and a number of bowel disorders. It is remarkable, medically speaking, that most of us function as well as we do.

Probably quite as important are the practical difficulties asocial societies place in the way of any attempt by the individual to adjust his relationships. Even in a highly organized society, some of the ill effects of anxiety can be offset by the ability of the public to create a limited stability at home. But the militarism and public hysteria of present-day city cultures, and their steady drift towards a permanent war economy, make escape of this kind precarious. Conscription, physical

separation, lack of privacy and comfort resulting fr
current war, and above all, during the intervals of recuperatiᴜ.
the growing conviction of individuals that anything they build
is bound to be destroyed by a repetition of the sequence,
militate so strongly against any attempt at stable relationships,
sexual or otherwise, that the effort seems useless. A permanent
war economy, whether open and of the fascist pattern or of the
veiled 'cold war' type that shows signs of coming into existence
in democratic countries, not only impedes normal patterns of
sexuality – it precludes them, or it would preclude them were it
not for human resilience.

In spite of their overt anti-sexual bias, or more correctly,
perhaps, because of it, centralized urban societies produce a
heightened emotional tension that leads to a state of persistent,
because often unsatisfied, sexual excitement. The dissatisfaction
of the public with its personal experiences of sexuality is expressed in art and entertainment as an intensive preoccupation
with romantic love, with sexual success and with virility. The
impact of this atmosphere of anxious preoccupation on the
individual is seen in the growth of that form of advertising
which depends on the promise of sexual success, or the image of
'togetherness:' the stable permissive home life for which we
long in vain if our personality defects and those of the times have
prevented us from achieving it in fact. The more highly mili-
tarized societies sometimes engage in an intensive propaganda
for a higher birth rate, which is in direct conflict with the obstacles militarism places in the way of stable marriage, and
whose poor success surprises only the promoters. The competition between minimum outlet and maximum stimulation, fear
of sexuality and patriotic appeals for larger families, hindrance
of the normal and hatred of the abnormal, constitutes one of the
'vicious spirals' to which asocial societies are prone, and which
can propel them towards historical and social breakdown.

On the other hand – and this is where the Jeremiads fail to
square with reality, – the same society which has generated
'problems' has also generated opportunities, and the increased
density of the one only reflects the increased yield of the other.
The new respect of parents for their children's wishes, the new

equality of the sexes, the far greater range of individual choice, the growth of a civilized distaste for aggressive public and private policies, all these make for better living, but all impose an additional strain on us. If our society is anxious, that is at least in part because its members are seeking solutions for their problems by the exercise of their own judgement, rather than putting up with things as they are, or accepting the authority of tradition. As the creator of 'Flook' remarked, 'there's a great spirit of anti-bullying about: the sacred cows are within reach of the butchers'. Modern man is certainly finding it hard to adjust to the present high rate of social change, but the majority of him is not doing badly. If he can restrain a minority of psychopaths – many of them, unfortunately, in office, we may be on the verge, not of a bust-up, but of a break-through. In the field of rational sex relations, where individual initiative counts, this already appears to be happening; the much-abused younger generation may be teaching its elders, and psychoanalytical ideas might lead us to expect a revolution beginning here to spread throughout our more public institutions – a general turning-out of Thanatos, who now governs them, in favour of sociality, permissivity, and a lowering of tension. The only serious question is whether this can happen in time to prevent a breakdown of civilisation. My personal belief is that it can and will.

EXTENT OF THE SEXUAL PROBLEM [17, 18, 19]

The fact of having made sex into a 'problem' is the major negative achievement of Christendom. The 'problem' has become *vocal* in our present society, not because we are specially disturbed, but because we now recognize the defect in our attitudes and, under pressure of growing knowledge, we are trying to alter them. Our real need is for a mentality in which the word 'problem' is banished permanently in favour of 'enjoyment.' The essence of the 'problem' is that for many people and for various reasons enjoyment is lacking. So is security – and so too, very often, is love.

It is difficult to obtain any statistical picture of sexual inadequacy in the absence of reliable figures, and those conjectures which have been investigated statistically have, as a rule, proved wide of the mark. People sometimes appear indestructibly resilient: inadequacy is a clinical reality, but the surprising thing is that there is not more of it. Not long ago it was the fall in the birth rate that was attracting most attention, though this has proved to be a natural slump after an unnatural boom. The divorce rate is not in itself an index of the instability of marriage, since it is partly conditioned by changed ideas of respectability and by modifications in the law. The most convincing evidence in the thirties came from clinical practice. In a series of women attending a London gynaecological out-patient department, one in three had experienced no orgasm in marriage. Even excluding denials based on false modesty, this coincided with the fairly well-known incidence of 'genital hypoplasia', backache of obscure cause, dysmenorrhea, and other symptoms which are believed to be psychosomatic in origin. Estimates based on clinical data tend to be statistically unsound, because only the sick complain, and because many suffer in silence. Marital surveys have, on the whole, confirmed the view that, next to fear and repudiation of sexuality as essentially sinful, straightforward psychosomatic difficulties have so far played the chief part in sexual maladjustment.* If this is the case, the next generation might be expected to do rather better, for they are far less inhibited, and there are signs of a secular trend towards greater satisfaction at the physical level. These surveys, however, give no indication of the proportion of patients who owe their maladjustment to personality problems, and those who owe it chiefly to the direct effects of war and to the conscription and disorganization that accompany it. The most striking figures are those relating to juvenile delinquency, which by general agreement originates *en famille.*

* Some idea of the difficulty of assessing the factors which lead to unhappiness in marriage can be obtained from the study by Terman.[20] This investigation is a particularly instructive example both of the problems of sexual sociology and of the type of investigation which can be undertaken to solve them. Terman's conclusions refer to a limited American sample, and the causes of unhappiness in existing marriages may well differ from those which lead to legal dissolution or separation. The exact role of sexual ignorance and traumatic experiences is discussed: Terman assigns a rather less prominent place to defects in sexual knowledge and attitude than we have suggested – his other findings also differ from some of our conclusions and should be studied for comparison.

Juvenile delinquency is probably a reliable index of the instability of the family. In considering it, and the statements made about it by the indignant, certain corrections are necessary. We need to exclude certain forms of sexual 'delinquency' in juveniles, not because they are unrelated to family attitude, but because in contemporary Western societies no form of pre-adolescent sexual activity is accepted, or, more accurately, no form is universally accepted by all social groups. The fact that adults react defensively against the memory of their own pre-adolescent sexual history, and that medical men and psychiatrists are drawn from social groups in which pre-adult sexual outlets other than masturbation are at a minimum, makes it likely that a boy or girl of a low social group who engages in homosexual play with schoolmates, or even a girl who engages in 'petting' at an earlier age than usual, may be classed as a delinquent, or in need of protection, and segregated accordingly. Just as many forms of conduct which are reckoned as delinquent in adult subjects are probably statistically normal forms of behaviour, so sexual delinquency in children is not always a direct measure of sexual deficiency in a society; the conflict is less with sociality than with a miscalculation by society itself. This caution is necessary, in view of the tendency in some sections of the literature to regard juvenile sexual delinquency as a special index of moral collapse. The general pattern of juvenile delinquency, however, and a very large part of non-delinquent behaviour found in groups which have grown up in the asocial background, is of great importance.

The human being is born at a very early stage of development by comparison with other mammals. He is dependent on parental care for a far greater proportion of his average life than any other higher animal. During this period his normal social and intellectual development depends almost wholly on the stability of the family and on the dynamics of the relationships which exist within it. Failure of these produces a personality which is itself incapable of responsible social attitudes. The family is a uterus from which the child must not be expelled until gestation is over. (This is really the biological kernel of sexual morality). Delinquency as we know it, whether it assumes forms of which the law takes cognizance, or whether it is of the more dangerous kind which manifests itself in aggression, the desire for dominance over others, unreasoning patterns of behaviour, and irresponsible conduct through and within existing conventions of behaviour, is a form of prematurity. It is also one of our chief endemic diseases.

Halliday[2] writing in 1946, illustrated this process in relating the increases in psychosomatic disease to the changes in adult and infant environment since 1870. He relates parental and child anxiety to the fertility rate as follows, the 1960 figure being an attempt at prophecy which sticks to query marks (in the event, fertility has risen and child anxiety probably declined, but there is no numerical scale by which such estimates can actually be judged).

	PARENT	CHILD	FERTILITY RATE (per cent)
1870		+	100
1900	+	++	−25
1930	++	+++	−59
1960	+++	(?)	(?)

The main factors in this progress he divides as follows: 'increasing separation from outward roots in earth', 'increasing disregard of biological patterns', 'increasing frustration of manipulative creativity', 'increasing standardization and repression of individual expression', 'decreasing sense of aim and direction'. The coercive, religious, and economic features of Victorian civilization have left their mark on a generation of parents and in the obsessional traits of their children – partly, it seems, by way of the impact on childhood of the ritualistic cleanliness which has replaced the older squalor. Halliday comments, though without statistics, on the marked increase in 'chastity' among the troops of 1940, as compared with those of the Boer war, which may in itself represent a shift of normal sexuality into less normal channels; one might go on to say that there is evidence that such a shift, if real, represents an extinction of the more normal kinds of sexual delinquency in favour of the less normal, asexual kinds, comparable to the strange chastity of many of the prominent delinquents of history.

Sex in Society

This is a typically well-intended and in the main, sensible, prediction of 'disaster-unless'. Such predictions are, fortunately, rarely realized. It is clear that the instability of an asocial order is self-propagating, through its results on the family. In particular, the mechanism of asocial cultures, by giving abnormal scope to the aggressive psychopath who can attain office, leads it to collect in its governments, its armies, its bomb-constructing programme, and the staff of its machinery of enforcement, individuals who exhibit the desire to dominate irresponsibly the lives of other people. It has been frequently suggested that asociality or its products, such as totalitarian war, play a large part in producing abnormal sexual conduct – 'perversion', in its current sense. Probably it only facilitates their expression. The patterns of acceptable and inacceptable sexual conduct vary considerably in different social groups, but there is evidence that in each group they are remarkably stable and resistant to change. It is possible that the growth of asociality, by hindering normal outlets, has precipitated abnormal ones in many individuals, since home instability bears a definite relationship[22] both to prostitution and to some forms of atypical behaviour, such as homosexuality and exhibitionism. Permitted aggression in our society is rare – we are in general far more civilised than our forebears. But aggression is there all right, and its outbreak may account for many of our behaviour patterns, from suicide to hooliganism. These patterns seem in practice to result from the failure of the normal aggressive 'drive' to find suitable material upon which to work. Freud himself postulated a 'death-instinct' to explain them – others put them down to frustration of more positive drives.

> The individual must be vouchsafed the opportunity to gratify the life-instinct of providing food, shelter, and the release of the sexual urge in socially acceptable ways. Otherwise frustration may fortify the death-instinct. . . . Suicide and all manifestations of masochism derive from the death-instinct. So do homicide, war, and that complex of aggressions known as the sadistic impulse. Love in all its sexual connotations springs from the life-instinct. . . . The ascendancy of either one spells life or death for the individual.—A. J. LEVINE.

The Social Background and Its Problems

Some of this hostility is discharged in behaviour we would now recognize as sadistic: its sexual content may vary widely, while remaining linked to the component of unresolved aggression. The frankly sexual manifestations of sadism and masochism, while they may exceptionally result in murder or violence to a sexual partner, are most commonly expressed as fantasies. They are a prominent feature of the art and entertainment of all asocial groups, either as a fascination with particular symbols, such as floggings, fetters, torture, and violence, or in the prevalance of dangerous sports and spectacles: gladiatorial shows in 'suicide' motor-races, both of which play a part in the history of centralized urban cultures far greater than can be explained in terms of the demand for physical excitement, and there is violent disagreement between those who argue that simulated violence helps us to get such impulses out of our system, and those who believe that a diet of murder can corrupt by precept and example (the two views are not mutually exclusive). But sexual fantasies of this kind, and the less obviously sexual manifestations of sadism, do tend to become important in all such societies as a means of government. The growth of atrocity propaganda is of interest in this context. An atrocity, in the sense in which the word has been lately employed, is not only a barbarous action but one having specifically sexual overtones. The public to whom an atrocity story is directed reacts primarily not by indignation but by sexual excitement. This excitement is of a kind which few individuals are able to admit to themselves, and they react consciously by indignation against the alleged perpetrator. It is noticeable that many of the fictitious atrocities of belligerent propaganda during the 1914 war, such as the German corpse factory, were enacted in fact by the combatants of 1940. Both the stories and the facts sprang from a general reservoir of sadistic imagery and reaction that was present, and has greatly increased in magnitude, within Western cultures during that period.

Personal violence in daily life, in spite of crime waves, teddy boys and the other show pieces of the preacher, is actually less in evidence now than ever before in our history, if we exclude traffic accidents from the definition. Some of the violence which

59

there still is, moreover, and which erupts to shock the citizens, is not the product of sadism so much as of exasperation. Modern society *is* exasperating in spite of being prosperous and comfortable for the fortunate – and it is the fortunate who are tending to erupt rather than the homeless, the unemployed or the misfit. The irritant is sometimes said to be 'lack of social purpose' – but the classical symptom of exasperation, namely explosive and undirected violence by relatively well-off youngsters who are not certain what it is they want to smash, is found both in Bingo-land and in the Marxist states, where 'social purpose' is as present as in wartime democracy, and probably as facile. 'Asociality' is a vaguer term – implying life at a level where a human vitamin is missing, or where communication is somehow incomplete.

It is possible to over-emphasize the importance of 'sadistic' symbols in literature, and even well-marked sadistic impulses confined to the strictly sexual field do not generally cause delinquent behaviour in otherwise sane persons, any more than all greedy people become pathological misers. But such impulses readily lose their connection with coitus and replace it in whole or in part. In different individuals they may give rise to types as dissimilar as the fanatical disciplinarian, the flogging schoolmaster, the prison-camp guard, or the reformer who is unusually sensitive to the evils of cruelty. The last of these manifestations represents the most acceptable outlet of all irrational aggression – its diversion against objects which should, on rational grounds, be abolished. Aggression with sexual overtones is equally present in such apparently pointless activities as slashing seat-cushions in trains. But the growth of institutional militarism has given the other, and more dangerous types of reaction, a place in the system of power-society which makes them indispensable to authority, and which leads to their active encouragement. In a society where personal frustration is wide-spread, any form of aggressive behaviour which is socially acceptable will satisfy a widespread demand. The desire of hostility to inspire fear is satisfied by the requirement of authority for those who will help it to inspire fear as a means of government. As a result, asocial societies, which display the utmost disapproval and incomprehension towards other sexual deviations of limited public importance, and are ashamed to behave aggressively in private, tend to encourage hate in the interests of order and political power. In the tough guys of politics, and in the 'strong men' of dictatorial orders, we have examples of the diversion of abnormality into channels which permit it to be expressed in an accepted form. While mechanisms of this kind are detectable in almost all societies, the centralized pattern of modern life exaggerates them and renders their influence greater, and potentially more destructive, than in primitive cultures. It is likely that a scientific study of the real nature of antisocial behaviour may make us revise our entire attitude to the conception of responsible power; not only are dictatorships likely to throw up abnormal individuals, but the psychical mechanisms that lead individuals to offer themselves for positions of power in a social democracy are themselves found to belong increasingly to the field of psychopathology. The atomic bomb, like the gallows and the concentration camp, is yet another cathectic idea 'gone wrong'. Its political proprietors have this much in common with the rapist or the swindler: its scientific advocates have been caught faking results to make a political point.

> Although there are many habitual criminals who specialize in using the mails to defraud, there are many others who have been convicted of this offence who are not essentially different in their psychological make-up from the average candidate for public office. The promises of over-sanguine inventors, mining-stock promoters, and a large number of brokers are of the same timbre as those of the candidates for Congress or for governor who secure votes on the strength of promises they can never fulfil.[23]

Asocial societies can drift into militarism because they pass out of their own control. The modern form of military barbarism as we saw it in Fascism, or even a democracy in war time, leads finally to these chief sexual consequences: it abolishes marriage by interference with personal life; it puts a premium on social abnormality and physical disability; and it leads to a chronic sub-anxiety state in the decreasing population of civilians that ultimately renders normal family relationships impossible. (Oddly enough, a 'democracy' at war is in one compensatory sense *more* social than in peace – it acquires a common object, and neurosis may actually decline for the duration of the emergency: the effects of family disruption only appear later on.) In practice, many individuals are already feeling the consequences of this process. A social order based on the preparation for, and fear of, war, even excluding the occurrence of war itself, is in itself highly destructive to individual security. The pattern of accepted 'normality' is probably unaltered, but the capacity for its expression in daily life is impaired.

It is possible to relate the increase in delinquent and antisocial behaviour even more closely to the general pattern of our society. Individual standards of conduct depend on parental attitude – up to the age of puberty the parent is the child's external conscience, who is loved as a source of security and hated as a restrictive influence. After puberty, conduct depends on the functioning of the individual's own body of standards (ego-ideal), and of the force that compels conformity to these standards, an aggregate which consists of social *mores*, ethical ideas, and largely irrational fears and restrictions intimately mixed. When the individual accepts the orders of a central authority, a military command, or a political organization, for instance, he passes on the responsibility for his actions to the group, which becomes, for him, a second parent. At the same time, the actual attitude of this fictitious parent will be determined by those individuals who display the most aggressive attitude towards others, the 'men of action' who gravitate to the top of the hierarchical pyramid. Some external standards, provided by belief in God or reverence for parental teaching, may well be concrete expressions of the individual's own moral outlook, but the dictates of the political or military super-ego depend on the decisions of single fallible and ambitious individuals: these tend to become the standards of entire nations and to shape the national conscience.

The tendency displayed by fascism and communism, under

which unanimity is demanded and military training begins at or before puberty, is evident in all highly centralized orders, even when it has not reached the same lengths. As a result, the 'male' unit, the military group and its discipline, takes over from the parental authority before the end of character formation, and the child is not permitted the opportunity of developing personal responsibility.* The continuance of an externalized super-ego into adult life accounts for many of the social features of fascism; in less regimented societies, where the same process exists, but the external conscience is itself contradictory and indefinite, as it is in England today, the product may be an adolescent and adult delinquency at a personal level, which is the counterpart of the group delinquency of totalitarian states. In urban America a similar problem seems to arise from different causes and takes the form of an enormously prolonged adolescence, owing to the absence in city aggregates of a coherent society into which the child can graduate. The ideals of the group may prove so wildly at variance with the normal standards inculcated by education that an adult moral outlook may fail to emerge at all.

Both totalitarian and non-totalitarian urban orders tend to produce individuals with separate public and private faces, the sadistic SS man who is genuinely attached to his family, the politician of 'great private integrity' who orders the indiscriminate bombardment of civilian centres – this duality is, of course, not new, since it occurs in almost all societies as a suspension of responsibility towards outsiders, but it plays an important part in reconciling the difference between public and private standards, both in sexual conduct and elsewhere.

THE SEXUAL ATTITUDE OF ASOCIAL SOCIETIES

1. *Religious Tradition*

The sexual problems arising from the asocial pattern of living had to be faced by a public that was singularly ill

---

* I doubt from observation if this is equally true of Communism, i.e. contemporary Soviet Marxism. Unfortunately there is no room here for a longer exposition of personal theories – they have taken too much room already in a book on sexual behaviour.

equipped to deal with them, by reason of the attitude it adopted, and still adopts, toward sexuality. The false modesty of Victorian England can be traced to a number of systems of psychodynamic cause and effect, but it rested on a far older cultural and religious foundation.

Christianity presented to the growing civilization of Western Europe a body of philosophy and theology and a system of ethics that have profoundly influenced all our attitudes. In the heat of argument today, vigorous assertions are made both by the opponents of Christianity and by its supporters about the contributions to social ideas which originated in the Christian ideology.

All religions contribute positive elements to the cultures in which they grow. At their zenith they provide mechanisms through which coherence and social unity are imparted to societies, and through which individuals can discharge, and receive absolution from, their own antisocial impulses. How far the Christian conception of the status of the individual has contributed to the progress of liberal humanism, and how far it has influenced our ideas of the equality of the sexes or the unity of the family, are debatable issues, since cultural causes and effects are not easy to identify, and Christianity itself has undergone a process of liberal transformation through the pressure of secular and anti-Christian viewpoints.

Some facts are, however, fairly distinct. Christianity has always placed the regulation of sexual conduct in the forefront of its ethical system. It has always relied, sometimes deliberately and sometimes unconsciously, on the calculated generation of sexual anxiety as a source of its authority. Indeed, no pornographer has ever 'exploited' sex so thoroughly. 'Christian teaching' must be held to comprise both the liberal ideas of Milton's *Tetrachordon* and the deep-seated anti-sexuality of a long tradition of virgins and celibates. In dealing with Christianity as an influence we are not dealing with the teaching or beliefs of its most intelligent or most liberal exponents,[69] and modern Christian ethical writers who point to the exaggeration of Christian anti-sexuality in psychological literature must face the reply that it is with the consequences on the public attitude toward sexual conduct, rather than on the intention of the teachers, that our estimate of Christianity as a socio-sexual influence must rest.

Whatever Christianity may have contributed to the growth of our culture in other fields, it seems undeniable that in sexual morals and practice its influence has been less healthy than that of other world religions. It assimilated many of the least liberal and human elements of Judaism, and the structure of power-society which originated in, and ultimately destroyed, the civilization of Rome. From these elements it created a system of sexual ethics and an attitude toward sexuality, at once rigid, antagonistic to the observed facts of human character and behaviour, and based upon fear, to which the imminent end of the world added point. The reform of this attitude has taken place only slowly and in step with the crumbling away of much of the structure of the older Christian ideology. This older ideology tends, however, to persist in modern Catholicism – it also persists to an alarming degree in the group mind. The reasons for the earlier flight from the problem of sexual ethics appear to have been the same as those which now threaten the pattern of Western cultures. Christianity emerged in, and spread as a reaction against, the asociality of Rome under the Empire; in fairness to the early Christian moralists it must be realized that in spite of the superficial sexual frankness of late Roman culture they never had the opportunity to observe the functioning of sexuality in a normally orientated society. The flaunting by Roman asociality of its sexual problems, the disgust of Jewish proselytes at the *mores* of a new Sodom, and the conception of an imminent Second Coming, which affected early Christianity much as the atom bomb affects many contemporary theorists, and provided a background against which personal relationships were devoid of meaning, all contributed to the excesses of early Alexandrine and Roman theology.

It is possible to overstate the effects of religious doctrine on group attitudes. In part, at least, they are as much products as causes of these attitudes, although they tend to perpetuate existing moral patterns. The attitudes of a given section of a society towards sexual behaviour, and the forms of behaviour it accepts, are based on systems of thought that are neither systematized nor fully conscious. The importance of these group attitudes lies in the fact that if they are transgressed, even in matters where they coincide neither with the law nor with the *mores* of other groups, they are a prolific source of guilt and personal conflict. In civilized as in primitive orders, these attitudes are among the attributes from which the individual finds it hardest to escape. The attitudes of ruling groups have profoundly influenced the presentation both of ethics and of scientific fact. There is a closely similar tendency today to treat the patterns of behaviour found in other social groups as abnormal, and to erect those of the writer's own background as a pattern for others.

In our own society, however, all groups share to some extent in the common negative attitude towards sexuality, which is, at least in part, the outcome of religious belief. In English society it is only the most educated levels, and these only recently and superficially, which have ceased to regard all sexual activity as a source of guilt, sin, and dangerously deep-seated emotions, and its expressions as basically dangerous and hostile acts. The unconscious attitudes of the public hark back to the manifest psychopathy of the Alexandrian monks, to the dictum of St. Anselm that woman is the torch of Satan, and to the concentration of all the moral energies in resistance to the seduction of the flesh. The current sense of the word 'immoral' is an index of the underlying attitude of this culture.

Another trait that exists prominently in Christian history is the emphasis on the value of suffering and self-abasement. The history of its doctrines and the circumstances of its foundation focused attention on pain and privation as means of atonement, but the deliberate seeking out of pain as a substitute for the claims of the flesh had no part in the earliest Apostolic teaching and seems to have originated in the asocial society of Roman North Africa rather than in the Jerusalem of Christ. This view of the merit of privation has become deeply ingrained in the belief of European cultures. Its place in the psychology of conduct, as we now know it, gives it a fundamental appeal to the sexually maladjusted. The ideas of atonement and suffering are most prominent in monotheistic religions, and appear to be related to the sense of guilt arising from infantile jealousy[24] most individuals feel towards their physical father. It is impossible either to discuss or to assess the psychoanalytical interpretation of religion in this book, but whatever the origin of the Christian praise of suffering, it shows fairly obvious historical associations both with deviant forms of sexuality and with the voluntary self-castration of the monastic system.

The net impact of Christian teaching over nineteen centuries upon the public mind in our own culture has produced several clear-cut assumptions: that of all moral delinquencies, sexual misdeeds are the most serious; that sexuality in itself is a trap, fraught with ritual and personal danger; that suffering, abstinence, and virginity are desirable as indices of moral value; and that right sexual conduct on the ethical plane is identical with the most suppressive *mores* of the group, not only in social matters, such as marital fidelity, but in details of custom, such as the avoidance of nakedness. At times it has been yet more equivocal – in its attempts, for example, to preserve unwanted pregnancy and venereal disease as sanctions to support its teaching.

It is unimportant that this system of belief no longer represents the teaching of intelligent Christians in most communities, and that Christian history contains many protests against it. The older and more deeply rooted attitudes persist, and the decline of the prestige of Christian belief has prevented any undoing by more modern ideas of religious morality of the results of the past. Religions of all kinds provide a mechanism by which many antisocial or repressed impulses may be worked out in harmless forms, but not even these palliative mechanisms persist today. The tendency of much Protestant moral teaching has been to reassert in terms of social science the standards it formerly taught in terms of revelation; the general position of Catholicism is fundamentally unchanged in sexual matters since the Middle Ages.

2. *Sexual Knowledge and Discussion*

The association in the public mind between sexuality and guilt is probably the most important single factor in the individual problems patients bring to marriage-guidance and psychiatric clinics. It is accompanied by a prevalent ignorance of fact, which is only slowly being remedied by popular education. Attempts to bring scientific attitudes to the rescue of older and irrational moral systems have confused the issue still further. Fear of the entirely illusory physical effects of masturbation still underlies a proportion of neurosis in young men; this fear is traceable almost entirely to books and pamphlets dating from the mid-nineteenth century, many of which are unfortunately still in print. In all branches of health education, the refutation of fallacies takes longer than the spreading of new knowledge.

The Victorian attitude towards masturbation could hardly have persisted in the presence of free discussion between individuals of their own sexual experiences. This component of solitariness plays a very large part in the production of sexual anxiety. In contemporary society, the sexually anxious individual is above all *alone*, even more than the neurotic who fears what his neighbours may surmise about his symptoms and sanity. He has no idea how others behave, whether his own conduct resembles theirs, or whether his impulses are a sign of disease and depravity. In lower social groups, where discussion is more open and privacy less complete, the solitude of the individual is less rigid; but the middle classes undergo a type of psychological solitary confinement in the company of their problems. Medical men, derived from the same class, do not always receive with willingness or with adequate knowledge the attempts of the prisoner to share his difficulties; the teaching of psychology and sexual hygiene is inadequate or absent in most English medical schools, and such attempts frequently lead to a rebuff that further discourages repetition.

One curious result of this isolation has been the dropping out from middle-class language of the entire vocabulary of sexual instruction and of excretion, which is linked with it in individual development and in the canon of decency. As a token of respectability, this verbal censorship has spread into all social strata in their dealings with the doctor.

A serious deterrent to free discussion of sex matters in marriage between doctor and prospective entrants, except those of the more educated classes, is the candidate's ignorance of simple anatomical and physiological terms. Whatever the Old Kent Road's equivalents of 'vagina' and 'orgasm' may be, the inhabitants are shy of using them to the doctor.

In America, marriage-guidance workers start by establishing a vocabulary of terms, the use of which relieves both sides of embarrassment; simple line-drawings are also helpful. It is better for the applicants for guidance to spend a little time learning a few words and facts than for the doctor to try to work with slang words which may be unfamiliar to the more genteel cases of Walworth.[25]

In the most educated groups there are signs that psychological teaching is taking the place of taboos, but in the form rather of rationalization of old attitudes than of accurate knowledge. The sexual practices within the range of normal variation which appeal to many individuals appear bizarre, and are a source of fear, to those who can identify them in Krafft-Ebing without having any further information about their significance. The reading of medical literature by laymen always spreads alarm and despondency. Bearing in mind the extreme oddness of most sexual behaviour, dispassionately viewed, this is hardly surprising, but it has considerable repercussions in the individual mind, and between husband and wife. Evidence of these repercussions can be found in many divorce hearings, as much as in clinical psychiatry, Thus we have seen that the play element in courtship probably bears the same relationship to deviant impulses as childhood play bears to childhood aggression. Such acts as struggling, slapping, tying, play-acting and dressing-up, may figure in both child-play and love-play. They are far too often cited in divorce courts as evidence of abnormality. In one of Norman Mailer's novels we find a drawing, apparently from life, of a couple who play a little scene to enliven each act of intercourse – they are by turns housewife and ice man, schoolgirl and seducer, odalisque and sultan. Such regressive goings-on worry us – we are apt to wonder what a psychiatrist would say about them. A good one would probably point out that adults need play as much as children, and that we lose something when we can no longer play at cowboys or kings. One would be more concerned at the abnormal significance of such adult play if the scenarió were more stereotyped – adults are shyer about being caught playing than are children, but they may need such outlets as much, if not more, while sexual intercourse is one of the few contexts which suspends their self-consciousness enough to make such psychodrama possible.

3. Censorship

The prisoners of their own fears and questionings have a possible avenue of escape in the written word and in the literatures of other cultures. The study of its literature is a useful guide to the degree of sexual security existing in a culture. There does not appear to be any record, however, of a power-society in which some form of institutional sexual censorship has not existed. The absence of the physical expression of sexuality is a striking characteristic of English literature between 1850 and 1900 and accurately reflects the attitude of the period. The existence of sexual censorship has its original roots, perhaps, in the fear of primitive animism that sacred and powerful words might bring national calamities if taken in vain, and in the revival of Oedipal anxieties in ill-adjusted members of the group. Sexual censorship in institutional societies, however, follows the same pattern as sexual law in reflecting an attitude more repressive and limited than that of any single group. It is not possible at the present time to reproduce in print the conversation of large sections of the public.

Recent history has produced types of censorship directed against three main threats to the security, first of the group ethic, and later of the individuals who control the institutional pattern: criticism of power and of institutions, criticism of religion, and open discussion of sexuality. The first two forms of restriction are common political features of most societies and tend to vary with the character of government. In recent years the first has largely replaced the second; the last, in its political form, seems to have arisen partly because of a half-conscious conviction among the holders of power that liberty of sexuality is in some way related to political liberty, and partly in the zeal of ruling classes to assert the supremacy of their own moral fibre.

Such groups, with some exceptions, have tended to regard rigidity in sexual morals as a commodity not for home consumption, but the emergent middle class of the post-Industrial period both maintained and observed the standards of sexuality embodied in its censorship. In asocial societies of the later type, waves of public anxiety are likely to be followed by waves of moral indignation, and by a clamour for the suppression of sexual literature, which originates sometimes in emotions closer to those of the animist, sometimes in distrust of the exponents of sexual reform, as enemies of the tribal magic, and sometimes, it appears, in more deliberate political diversionism. While, at the time of the first English revolution, prudery tended to be coupled with reformism and to become the standard of the emerging ruling class, sexual reform in the post-Industrial society has been largely identified with revolutionary attempts against that class, such as Marxism and Radicalism, or against its *mores*, such as rationalism and secularism; this fact has underlain the paternal attitude of censorship towards books intended for general reading. In the famous case of *R.* v. *Charles* (1935) a scientific textbook was suppressed not for its content but for the likelihood that, in a cheap edition, it would be available to the working classes. The Cockburn Rule, that obscenity in literature consists in the likelihood that matter will corrupt or deprave those open to such influences, 'beat the compulsory education act by a few months'.* The advent of revolutionary Marxism to power has tended, in Russia, to reverse the roles of reformer and conservative, and the increase in institutionalism to run parallel with a return of denunciatory comment against politically dissident obscenity. One striking

* Craig, A., *The Banned Books of England.*

feature of fascism has been its tendency to exhibit as much zeal in putting down indecency as did Victorian industrialism, coupled with a public encouragement of promiscuity as a token of racial health. Sexual studies, identified with public enemies such as libertarianism or the Jews, were severely treated, twelve thousand books from Hirschfeld's library being burned by the Nazis in 1933, and homosexuals consigned to concentration camps, in spite of the growth of homosexuality among the officer caste, an effect that is typical of military civilizations.

When normal sexuality is banished from literature, its place tends to be taken by a characteristic type of writing, which is correctly termed pornography. Genuine pornography is to the erotic literature of sexually balanced cultures as prostitution is to marriage: it is a substitute for more concrete satisfactions, a projection of sexuality into another medium, which may be explicitly sexual or not. Civilized cultures produce little pornography of this type and regard it as a condiment. Asocial cultures produce much and employ it as a diet. To the extent that pornography is such a substitute, the content of the majority of modern films, and even the violence that has invaded literature and art in non-sexual contexts, are pornographic, while, in the background that produced them, the ribald stories of writers like Boccaccio or Chaucer are not. 'Ours may not be a particularly lustful age, but it is a sexually irritated age.'[68] The audience to whom these earlier works were addressed is unlikely to have experienced great stimulation in reading them, while the Motion Picture Association's Code, although it precludes references to normal sexuality, has not succeeded in freeing films from an intense and abnormal erotic atmosphere. The history of pornography in asocial cultures is one of progressive deviation away from the celebration of love and pleasure toward outlets more and more abnormal and more and more divorced from genital sexuality. The erotic art of asocial cultures and their public entertainments deal chiefly not with love, but with hate and aggression, and are very largely tinged with pornography of a kind which censorship actively favours. By contrast, the art of the illegal pornographer, if one can call it that, consists largely in introducing in lawful, edifying and even devout abnormality the element of normal sexual reference which will make it sell to normal people.

The odd oversight which left Latin and Greek in our school curricula has ensured that no precautions have ever quite cut Englishmen off from literature which celebrates the physical experience of sexuality. It has been easier to keep them in ignorance of traditions which celebrate it visually, giving it the place traditionally occupied in our own iconography by the celebration of deprivation and pain. With the growing contact between Western and Eastern traditions which has followed the end of colonial rule in India, we now have increasing access to one such tradition, that of medieval Hindu sculpture. The shock effect of the erotic subjects in this art on Europeans was no part, certainly, of the artist's intention; it is not unlike the shock-effect on Asians of their first encounter with the sadistic topics of Christian iconography, which to us are now only decorative. The emotions produced by the depictions of coition in Hindu temples and of execution in our own are in fact homologous but opposite. They idealize genital pleasure as we have idealised death and barrenness. A Hindu may have difficulty in understanding art in which mother and child are the conventional symbol of virginity, but he will be familiar with asceticism – European taste, however, has banished genital sexuality altogether, and is now experiencing the need to regrow a self-amputated limb.

The trade-mark of our art has in fact been the exclusion, not of sexuality, but of genitality. In one sense, this lopsidedness is factitious, and the impression given by our libraries and galleries is false. Such art is not absent from our experience because nobody has produced it, but because it has been suppressed, destroyed, or concealed by an active minority bent on seeing we did not get it – a far more curious phenomenon that its absence would have been, for the suppression did not reflect the taste or the *mores* of the culture as a whole.

The natural history of sexual satisfaction and of human sexual behaviour is in fact now reappearing in our art. It has ceased, or is ceasing, to be shocking or incongruous, and we are becoming able to observe and describe this long-forbidden section of daily experience as D. H. Lawrence could not – that is, naturally and without strain. In visual art we have fewer precedents (I suspect from the work of Resnais and others that its natural medium may turn out to be the film) and Hindu art is too far out of our culture to provide models. We might usefully look at it, however, to find out the social functions which erotic art discharges in cultures which encourage it: they are of considerable interest to aesthetic biology.

The erotic art of the Hindu temples is primarily didactic. Its exact place in the religious life of the makers is disputed, even by modern Hindus, but the culture which produced it draws no very rigid distinction between sacred and secular. What is presented is an experience, edifying, practical and symbolic, of the way of Release which is the Hindu ideal, embodied in one form of Release, the contemplation of art. Another mode of Release is the experience of sexual ecstasy. The lovers of the *maithuna* groups both celebrate and demonstrate this: they are also symbols of the union of Mind and Nature, or of Immanence and Energy, but these meanings are accessory to their erotic meaning – they stimulate our desire for this sort of Release in exactly the same way that a flower show stimulates our wish to have gardens.

This, in all probability, is what secular erotic art would do in our own culture if disturbed people did not prevent it. The appeal of sexual representations in art is only limited to the 'corrupt', or their modern descendants the 'immature', if human beings generally are corrupt and immature. Large numbers of people want them (if they did not, such energy would not have to be spent in suppressing them) for reasons as worthy as those which produce a literature of ballroom dancing, plus one other – their power to evoke psychophysical excitement directly. This is the factor the prohibitors emphasize, because they are upset by their own response to it – they represent it as socially dangerous and artistically unworthy, preferring art to exploit the only subject which evokes an equal physical response namely violence. Love is corrupting and dangerous – violence is cathartic and wholesome, besides being politically useful.

Although people undoubtedly do seek out sexual art in our

society to experience excitement, they seek it equally for re-assurance. Part of the popularity of sexual literature today is due to a widespread conviction that knowledge is being kept from us which would make for greater proficiency and enjoyment in our own experience: part is the result of legitimate curiosity, the desire to compare our habits with other people's and be liberated from the anxieties which alloy our experience of Release.

Visual erotic art, however, has a special and a deeper significance, because it acts directly on the human response to sexual dimorphism associated with the Oedipal fears. Reassurance against the castration fear may perhaps be one of the original motives of representational art, and the manufacture of amulets against it the oldest use of figure carving. It is this function which makes the artist the traditionally-licensed *voyeur*, and which dictates the oddly selective modesties imposed on him at different periods. It is probably behind many other aesthetic phenomena, ancient and modern, including the flight of modern art into non-representational techniques.

Hindu art is here didactic in a special sense, quite apart from the part which genital symbolism plays in its belief. The temple-builders capitalized the human Oedipal responses as a source of cultural energy – we do the same, but in the reverse sense. Their ideology got its motive power from the resolution of the Oedipal fear, ours from the anxiety it generates. Permission and incitement to carry a similar pre-Adamic freedom into sexual relationships are the precautions such a culture must take against individual doubts – censorship and the maintenance of private sexual anxiety are our precautions to preserve the contrary adjustment against individual wishes.

What we know of the psychology behind the wish to prohibit sexual art makes it difficult to view such attempts with any more indignation than other sexual disabilities, such as fetishism or homosexuality. This one is unfortunately distinguished, however, by the desire to impose itself on others. We have to recognize the rights of sexually squeamish people – they are entitled to ask that things which upset them should not be forced needlessly on their notice: they deserve in this the same

consideration we give to those who (for identical unconscious reasons) are upset by pictures of surgical operations or
of snakes. But unfortunately, since there is no object, from hair
to table-legs, which the human mind cannot sexualize, these
demands invariably spread, and the point is reached at which
we are obliged to tell those who make them to look the other
way if our art offends them. In the case of written matter
there can be no such excuse, for a book stays closed until it is
opened, and it can be voluntarily closed at any moment. The
possible effects of sexual representations on children need to be
considered – in general they are less likely psychologically to
cause trouble than the illustrations in a normal textbook of
surgery, which we probably keep for an adult audience. As to
the attempts of interested parties to maintain upon moral
grounds censorships which are really political, or of religious
bodies to stimulate sexual anxiety as a means of increasing their
own authority, they can only be resisted. It is a peaceful re-
venge of the Indian temple builders that a modern European
psychiatrist or biologist may be more at ease spiritually with
the iconography of Khajuraho and Bhuvaneshwar than that of
Chartres, more able to give intellectual assent to the four faces
of Siva and the beauty of the Apsaras than to the virgins and
thaumaturgists of our own tradition, imagery which he cannot
help recognizing as emotionally mischievous.

The conventional assertion – indeed, the legal definition,
under both the Cockburn Rule and the Obscene Publications
Act, is that pornography can or does 'corrupt'. If this means
that it does tangible psychological harm, the assertion might
be true if it specified what matter is harmful and to whom, but
we have no means of knowing this, for no study has ever been
published to demonstrate the ill effects of such matter, as the
ill-effects of guilt-centred hygiene literature have been demon-
strated, or those of violence in comic-books inferred.

The real truth is that pornography disturbs – it is, in fact,
matter having a sexual cast which some person is for the time
being attempting to suppress. 'Corruption' plays no real part in
the process – books on housebreaking might 'corrupt' potential
burglars, and under the wording of the present, revised, law,

they could be prosecuted as pornographic, but we all know they will not be. Murder does not disturb the would-be censors. Normal coition does. That is the real lesson of the campaign against Lady Chatterley. If she had been disembowelled under erotic but less explicit circumstances, that would not have been liable to corrupt us, whereas coition might.

4. Venereal Infection

The introduction of syphilis into Europe by the crew of Columbus's expeditions was perhaps the greatest godsend to the religious conception of sexual morality, history could possibly have provided. Since it arrived, God, the spirochete, and the unwanted baby have been firm allies in saving us from ourselves. Venereal disease had been known to the Greeks, but it had not constituted a risk severe enough to restrict the freedom of the Hellenistic sexual tradition. Now, at a single blow, that freedom was destroyed, For the first time the hierarchical conception of the sinfulness of sexuality received a physical and inescapable sanction. Syphilis, like the code of ecclesiastical morals, was no respector of persons. It visited its wrath to the third and fourth generation, making no distinction between the innocent and the guilty, between the single act inspired by passion and the life of irresponsible licence, and from the time of its arrival it has remained as a major bar to the rational reshaping of morals. For this reason, many previous attempts to mitigate its extent or to reduce the risk of infection by public education have met with strenuous and explicit opposition from religious bodies, who sincerely regarded it as a divine judgement in favour of a morality with which it appeared so providentially consonant.

Although prolonged familiarity has reduced the virulence of the organism and increased the resistance of the public, this process of race immunization has not solved the problem. Syphilis was, in the first instance, the prize of conquest, and by an appropriate allegory it has been consistently spread by war. This process continues today, assisted by the disruption of social life, the persistent sense of isolation in urban societies, the growth of insecurity, and one of the important symptoms of insecurity, alcoholism. It is doubtful, however, whether the actual population incidence of syphilis has, in fact, increased by comparison with what we know of venereal infection in the city communities of the eighteenth century. In the past it has been propagated by organized prostitution; in our lifetime its chief sources of spread have been armies, whether allied or of occupation, defeated populations, populations undergoing the social stresses of war and lately the prosperous but aimless society which has followed. The period of unmentionability was ended largely by the requirements of military fitness rather than those of public health. At the present time we possess adequate prophylactic and curative means, and the purely medical side of the problem may be expected to improve. Public education in sexual hygiene may well play as large a part in this process as penicillin and chemotherapy, for we are now encountering resistant strains.

It is, in fact, highly important for sexual science to emphasize the social aspects of venereal infection, since the attitude of official opinion is likely to be one of welcome for any medical measure which offers to conceal the nuisance at a cheap rate. Any quick remedy would be most desirable, but public health is not the tranquil contemplation of public disease and we cannot accept the implication of the view that syphilis, like tuberculosis and malnutrition, is an inevitable consequence of inevitable war and social insecurity.

During the second World War the alarm caused by the incidence of venereal disease in the British Army led to a temporary effort to meet the threat by coercion,* but the results of compulsory treatment typified the failure of institutional orders when, like Gilbert's Executioner, they attempt to cut off their own heads. (As a matter of fact, prostitutes were a reserved occupation!). Measures of this kind, however predictably unsuccessful, are likely to prove more popular with political leaders than the radical reform of patterns of living. In this case, as in others, the palliative resources of medicine are likely to be wasted unless they can be accompanied by wider applications of social biology to society.

* Under a Defence Regulation since repealed.

5. *The Credit Balance*

I have deliberately emphasized the unsatisfactory features of modern sexuality, because, while gloomy estimates of public conduct are common, few such estimates contain any analysis of the factors at work. They are inclined to rely on appeals to traditional morality, or institutional measures such as censorship or reform of marriage law, or on strictly economic analyses of society, such as those derived from Marxism. There is also a tendency among publicists to discuss single consequences of asociality, such as war, as if they were prime causes of a moral decline, existing in themselves and having an independent status beyond the scope of society, like bad weather. Much medical writing on marriage guidance and sexual hygiene is severely handicapped by its attempts to provide scientific grounds for traditional patterns of behaviour, rather than to assess behaviour and its consequences as a basis for ethics. To deplore the extent of sexual imagery in advertising and literature and to attribute individual misconduct to it is a highly limited view of what is really going on. Mackenzie[26] recounts the story of a youth who contracted venereal disease as a result of the sexual stimulation experienced when he saw a pair of naked legs in a train and infers that a stricter control of costume might help in restoring stability. The prevalence of this sort of comment justifies a fairly extensive statement of the place of sexual problems in the general picture of society, if only to emphasize that traditional patterns cannot be restored, even if they were desirable, and that clamour for prohibitory legislation is itself the obverse of over-excitement at a normal stimulus. In a society of informed people, which regarded sexuality as a feature of normal living and nudity in a reasonable light, it would be ludicrous to attribute 'immorality' to such stray stimuli, or, indeed, to any of the other single factors which masquerade as causes in the minds of irrationally motivated reformers.

If the sociological outlook as presented by moral and ideological meteorologists is depressing, it has a number of features which make it perfectly clear that a time of difficulty is also a time of opportunity. There is already reason to think that we are over the hump, and that so far from asocial societies turning all our sexual responses into neurotic and destructive courses, the human desire for love and pleasure may be about to reform asocial society, or to play a key part in doing so. It is quite unjustifiable to assume that asociality is bound to work itself out, or that faulty patterns of thought cannot be corrected in adults. Historical processes are by no means inevitable, though they require very concentrated effort to alter them, and there is nothing in Freudian theory to justify the view that adults are ineducable.

The most promising indications in the field of sexual sociology are the enormous resistance of humanity to asocial patterns, the growth of rational knowledge and its application to sexual ethics, and the appearance of public demand for better things. If the gloomiest sociological assessment were our only guide, we should expect to find no normality of family or personal life persisting, rather than a widespread prevalence of handicaps. One can only wonder, not that individuals encounter the problems which they do encounter, but that a high percentage of the population adjusts itself satisfactorily. Social behaviour is too deeply rooted in the pattern of human thought for it to be eradicated even by several decades of asociality in its most extreme forms, such as fascism; and it persists, not only in groups such as prisoners, isolated communities, and dispossessed elements such as outcasts and racially oppressed minorities, who have a way of rallying which shames the more privileged, but also potentially in the general public; if this can be released it will by itself lead to the reformation of the asocial order. It is obviously a slow and costly method of dealing with asociality to wait for this spontaneous collapse – our own generation, in spite of its defects, has unique technical and intellectual equipment to bring about the necessary changes intentionally. For the first time in the history of any comparable society, social behaviour is now the subject of exact study, based on observation, and such a study is in itself highly resistant to interference by power. We cannot assume any false security when there has been one major attempt already to do away with psychoanalysis as a 'Jewish science', but the fact remains that knowledge, though it can be suspended, is now very nearly indestructible. Even the cynicism of the public towards political institutions is only the negative aspect of a constructive desire for fuller living and for responsible normality.

The opportunities offered to the individual are also unique – the possibility of regulating conception and of controlling venereal disease makes it feasible to examine modes of sexual behaviour for the first time in themselves, so that we can determine their desirability on rational grounds, and without reference to accidentals or to non-rational moral systems, while technology and hygiene render the aesthetic and recreative aspects of sexuality accessible to larger and larger sections of society. These opportunities do not outweigh the problems of asociality, but they offer a major incentive for a concerted effort towards a rational and healthy individual life.

Any success in bringing about such a change will depend upon a realization by psychiatry both of what is wrong and of the responsibilities of medical science. There has been a tendency, reinforced by the war, for advisers to regard adaptation as an idol to which both the doctor and the patient should bow down, and rebellion or discontent as an indication of mental instability. In deciding whether to foster or discourage such discontent we have to examine the society to which the patient is being adapted – acquiescence in war, tyranny, or a negative attitude towards life is in itself pathological. Moreover, the aggressive impulses fostered by asocial living can be usefully employed only if they are redirected against the asocial pattern itself, rather than against external political enemies upon whom they are now focused, and against whom official or military psychiatry is obliged, by its terms of reference, to direct them. Psychiatry cannot legitimately be employed to stifle normal impulses toward peace and freedom; it must be prepared to accept the responsibility for encouraging individuals to modify society to suit man, not man to suit an arbitrary or irrational standard. It is incorrect to regard such activity by social psychologists as an importation of politics into medicine: sociology can be said to supersede politics insofar as it can give authoritative information on the way in which societies function, and its position in attacking the traditional ethics of political power, as well as those of sexual conduct, is comparable with the position of public health in attacking smallpox.

It is plain that a revolutionary denunciation of traditional institutions and attitudes may be, and often is, as much the product of unconscious forces as is a rigid assertion of tradition. It is possible, within limits, to predict the attitude which an individual will take up, if we are able to assess his personality type. To this extent, all branches of psychiatry have some justification for their unwillingness to commit themselves. It is, however, false to suppose that every revolutionary and rebel is by definition a psychopath, or that in a society which limits the potentialities of living and threatens the life and rights of the individual as profoundly as does our own, all protest is derived from purely personal conflict. Flugel,[29] whose masterly study of the psychology of the family has been much drawn upon in preparing this book, exemplifies the dangers of a strictly academic approach when he cites the opinion that strikes and unrest are commoner in the working- than in the middle-class because of the greater brutality of parental discipline which exists in low social levels! The caution with which the same author concludes that modern societies might profitably leave rather more room for individual initiative is commendable, but most people would be prepared to go further. The advent of psychopathic governments and, of psychopathic actions by governments, such as the concentration-camp system and the atomic bomb, have done much to emphasize the social necessity of individual disobedience; the ideas put forward on political grounds by early anarchists such as Godwin and Bakunin, or by the philosopher Kropotkin, are, it appears, more closely in harmony with the facts of human need and behaviour than any system which relies upon the continuation of centralized authority as we know it. Sexual ethics, in common with all other branches of social conduct, come under the scrutiny of this new standard of living, and the task of students in these fields is increasingly wrapped up with the need for a workable compromise between technical efficiency and personal initiative.

The Social Background and Its Problems

The concept of the free society is not a flight into the past or into a simpler order, but it does involve the recovery by technical societies of some, at least, of the positive attitudes of man, which have been lost during his development, to a point at which he can recover them by conscious effort.

Technology is indeed shaping some of our behaviour – contraception is an instance of a technique which could revolutionize it – but much that is written by scientists about the possibilities, e.g. of eugenics, of mass artificial insemination, of extra-maternal embryo rearing, and the like is more ingenious than sensible. Such techniques may quite well have applications occasionally (we need not be scared of them) but there is something a little pathological in the attempt to turn sex into a technological matter; the role of technology is surely to make its reproductive side more controllable and its play function more available. Even artificial insemination, which has given many childless couples their dearest wish, makes one wonder whether it has any advantage over the more traditional expedient of non-artificial insemination by a friend who is likely to go abroad shortly – possibly it has, but one senses the presence of those who would like to make all insemination artificial if they were only able to do so. Anthropological residues, too, have a surprising vitality after years of apparent dormancy. Primitive warriors abstain from coitus before battle for magical reasons. We criticize test cricketers who take their wives with them, for their lack of seriousness. In all our attempts to be rational, such apparent irrelevancies want watching – they can motivate us more than we realize, and play old Harry with our attempts to plan our attitudes by the light of reason.

The objective of sexual studies today is therefore fairly clear-cut – to determine, on a basis of factual research, the types of conduct best suited to the realization of mental and physical health, and to inform the public accordingly, both by ascertaining facts and presenting them, and by a co-operative effort with education and psychiatry to end the long-standing association between sexuality and guilt. Progress beyond this point, if we can get so far, will depend on other branches of effort, since the practical application of new ideas of

83

conduct will be possible only in a radically altered pattern of living; but in the forming of a reasonable society public conceptions of sexuality and the attitude of the public towards the family are bound to play a significant part.

One cannot predict what the outcome of present trends is likely to be, or how it will manifest itself socially. The threatening of individual health and values at all levels may in itself prove to be the main factor in bringing home to the individual the need for change based not upon institutional reform but on his personal acceptance of responsibility for his relationships, and on his disobedience to irrational patterns of authority.

IV

Monogamy and the Pattern of
Sexual Conduct

B EFORE sociology can answer the questions put to it whenever
sexual ethics are discussed, it must have some idea of the
type of sexual relationship it proposes to uphold as a generally
advisable pattern, allowing for individual differences, or, indeed,
whether it is going to uphold a generally advisable pattern at
all. In contrast to religious moralities, which attempt to cram
every foot into the same size of shoe, we are now more inclined
to stay quiet over what is 'generally advisable' and look only
at what seems advisable for a particular cluster of people at a
particular time. The analyst often goes further – being dedicated
to his own patient's interest, he is often obliged to assist him to
stop being excessively altruistic, or excessively guilty about his
lack of altruism, and so enable him to improvise.

Obviously, however, there are patterns which many individuals in our culture and with our background will find relatively
painless or rewarding, even if they cannot fit everyone. There is
a modal size of foot as well as a fashion in footwear. Beside this,
there is a pattern of mother-and-father relationship which is
virtually essential as a nidus for normal child development
(that other cultures have other patterns is hardly relevant: in
child-rearing one cannot set up a culture of one's own): there is
therefore a moral claim on those who have children to give
them the required nidus of security. These are the boundaries,
then, within which 'counselling', personal or by general exhortation, has to move. We are being asked what is in general
the wisest pattern of behaviour, exactly as we are asked what

85

most suitable general diet. So far we have referred to aspects of normality in individual behaviour, but not to ality in its social context. The emphasis of sexual studies and of psychoanalysis has tended to fall on deviations of impulse and on abnormal or exceptional sexual conduct. The social problems which behaviour of this kind raises are very largely creations of our own pattern of practice and attitude; the major part of human sexual activity falls within the system of the family, of the reproductive unit, as part of a permanent or semi-permanent personal relationship between adults.

A great deal of former and present controversy over the most desirable pattern of marriage has been based on argument from what is 'natural' – monogamy or polygamy have been cited as innate biological patterns in man. It is very doubtful whether anything can be learned by this approach. The types of sexual partnership in various societies and cultures have varied enormously and have clearly undergone extensive adaptation to fit other parts of the cultural pattern.[6, 27] The only serious question that requires an answer at the present time is whether, in the context of an industrial culture, permanent monogamy is or is not desirable. Any general advocacy of stable monogamy would have to be based on definite evidence that it is more satisfactory psychologically, and better adapted to the production of a stable environment for the rearing of children, than other types of relationship. In Bertrand Russell's words, we are substituting 'ends of life' for 'rules of conduct'. The answer we give to this question, unlike the answers of orthodox morals, cannot be taken as a categorical one – the personalities and staying power of individuals vary too widely for any such easy solution – and it will take the form of advice rather than condemnation or prohibition; but it is possible to say that the balance of evidence on all counts tells strongly in favour of some sort of monogamous pattern during the child-rearing period: arguments from child psychology have added force for a generation that recognizes the importance of home stability in forming the social attitudes of the child. We should try to examine the data that are available, and this involves a discussion of marriage in its present form, which is stable in centralized societies as a monogamous relationship recognized by the state, and the definition of the exact pattern of conduct which we are justified in advocating on scientific grounds. In any case, our ideas of the type of sexual relationship to be sought after and aimed at, and with which contemporary custom can be compared, must be based on general biological principles, not on averages drawn from the patterns that exist in primitive societies.

In terms of these general principles, it appears that a normal reproductive relationship has four major features. It is a voluntary relationship between adults, on a permanent basis, for mutual sexual enjoyment and for the foundation of a family. The essential points are the voluntary character of the relationship, the maturity of the parties, and the permanent and reproductive basis. In spite of the wide divergence of meaning attached to the word 'marriage', there is no other intelligible term for a relationship of this kind, and we can use it without accepting some, at least, of its current implications.

Much has been written about the selection of partners, and attempts have been made to trace resemblances between a man's mother and the woman he eventually marries, and to attribute compulsive attraction with a *déjà-vu* effect (what in less circumlocutory days was called falling violently in love at first sight) to recall of infantile memories. Some men may indeed be attracted to a woman who is like their mother, as artists are attracted by a particular 'type', but others, on Freudian grounds, would be equally likely to avoid her or prove impotent with her: infant memories are equally hard to prove, for the earliest of these would not be visual, but auditory or olfactory – that old pre-Freudian Groddeck did in fact suggest that 'in matters of love we let our noses decide for us'. All that can be said with reasonable certainty is that in some attributes, notably height and intelligence, people tend on the average to prefer mates who resemble themselves (assortation), and this becomes important if, and when, neurotics or psychotics are attracted by others with the same disability, or when a second marriage repeats the mistakes of a first. In other preferences infant memory, later conditioning, and even trifles like the sound of a name, can play a part, so that in all but the plainest cases our choices defy easy analysis. In this, our society differs radically from those which arranged their marriages on a commercial or kinship basis, or by order of a parent or the community: romantic love puts the whole responsibility for mate selection on the pre-conscious and unconscious mind, with minor help from the conscious reason – a system which has its drawbacks.

It is typical of the age that we write about sex, however, rather than about love, in this context – of the two, sex is the easier to identify, for love can be of many kinds. We use the term indiscriminately, to mean, compulsive attraction: the desire to possess another person or to enlist them in a fantasy of our own, which had far better be classified as cannibalism; and the genuine article, which is flavoured with both the preceding, but includes also mutual respect, mutual communication, and a strong desire to protect one another without any corresponding wish to manipulate or mould. Our society teaches that sexual relations spring naturally out of this kind of love – sometimes they do, but other societies, as Gauguin remarked, believe that this kind of love grows naturally out of satisfactory sexual relations, 'and who knows which view is the true one?' That they should be satisfactory is a *sine qua non* of real marriage, and since not only the psychological but the physiological sex endowments of individuals vary greatly, it seems sensible for the couple to establish a few of the parameters beforehand. There are risks of mistake in this too, however: a virgin rarely reaches her full sexual potential, and a man rarely displays his best performance, in a few hurried acts of pre-marital intercourse accompanied by anxieties about pregnancy, family disapproval, and other sources of conflict. In fact, in a really successful partnership sexual pleasure normally continues to increase in both parties throughout married life.

Legal marriage in modern societies has, of course, two aspects – a contractual and a moral, corresponding to the older civil and canon jurisdictions. It is only comparatively recently that marriage in England has ceased to be physically as well as morally coercive: until the Jackson case (1891) a husband had 'by law power and dominion over his wife, and may keep her by force within the bounds of duty and may beat her but not in a violent or cruel manner.' The attitude of the law has changed, but the contractual element is still prominent. 'There seems to be a prevailing impression that people who are unhappily married can come to the Divorce Court and ask that marriage be dissolved on that ground, but that is not the law. They took each other for better, for worse . . . and they must not expect that if the marriage falls short of their ideals they can get it dissolved. They may have to put up with a great deal of unhappiness. This Court does not intervene on grounds of unhappiness.'*

In laying down a social standard on public-health grounds we are not concerned either with the attempts of the state to regularize the pattern of marriage, nor with religious marriage, which is presumably a matter for the discipline of individual Churches and religious bodies. The law is of sociological importance only insofar as it does or does not coincide with patterns that are desirable on other grounds, and religious marriage insofar as it attempts to mould public opinion. The importance of both these factors lies in the fact that an institutional society relies on them, as institutions, rather than on the formation of a stable public attitude based on knowledge. The search for a biological norm excludes religious and administrative coercion, economic pressure, and social custom, and it deals with a relationship depending upon *mores*, not with an institution.

Modern societies have upheld monogamy on religious and legal grounds, but growing numbers of individuals have tended to accept a compromise between these official standards and varying degrees of promiscuity – a form of serial polygamy has become a serious competitor to monogamy as a pattern of marital conduct. The fact that religious teaching has centred its idea of marriage in coitus rather than in reproduction has further confused the issue, because the biological argument for monogamy is largely dependent on the existence of children. Infertile coitus has little or no social importance in the discussion of marriage. But from what we have said about the development

* Henn-Collins, J., 1945.

of the individual personality, it is clear that the stability or otherwise of the home in which childhood is passed is probably the most important single factor in character structure. Changes of parent and breaches of parental harmony have far-reaching effects on the child. It is therefore true, without reference either to the Church or the state, that from the point at which marriage is fertile it is 'indissoluble', to the extent that its dissolution may have harmful social effects.

It is important to recognize this, since some theorists appear to accept the religious valuation of coitus, and discuss marriage without reference to reproduction, by adopting an attitude based on adult inclinations rather than the significance of parenthood, and others transfer the entire religious conception of marriage bodily into scientific terms. As in other types of conduct, the foundation of marriage is a particular type of social responsibility, independent of external coercion, and flexible enough to allow for individual circumstances without dodging responsibilities. Relationships based on this kind of attitude bear no resemblance to licence – they were described by Iwan Bloch as 'free love' in contradistinction to 'wild love', though the term has acquired other implications through the frailty of its advocates and the malice of its opponents.

Opponents of the reproductive conception of marriage have tended to regard it as a matter *à deux*, to be arranged in terms of adult convenience. Reproduction is, however, a logical consequence of coitus, or at least an important and frequent sequel, and to ignore it is very like discussing diet without reference to nutrition. The advocates of 'wild love' grossly overestimate the efficiency of contraception, and even on those who specifically exclude the desire to produce children fertility is extremely likely to steal a march, often on several occasions. Until contraceptives can be devised which are foolproof, or unless we are prepared to be really efficient with existing measures, every act of coitus carries the specific implication of possible parenthood and must be viewed in that light. Unless great care is taken over contraceptive technique, therefore, the presence of an environment in which a child can be brought up, and brought up on a psychologically feasible basis, is a prerequisite of sexual intercourse between responsible adults. The rosy suggestions that have been made that in a sexually enlightened society children would be reared 'by the community', on the model of a few primitive societies, is at variance with what we understand of child psychology in our own pattern of culture: the idea that by the abolition of the family we should abolish the undesirable effects of the Oedipus situation would have no support from Freud, and might result in practice in a generation possessing no social orientation whatever, since the Oedipus situation is the foundation of positive moral attitudes as well as of neuroses. 'The profound and complex nature of the satisfactions which parents have in their children would very probably make the "communistic" rearing of children on a large scale as unsatisfying and inadequate from the point of view of the parents as it would probably be from that of the children themselves.'[29] A cogent answer to many of these arguments is to be found in the institutional child, and in the striking incidence of delinquency in children subjected to bandying about in infancy, at the time when they depend most upon stable emotional ties.

Impermanent sexual relationships, even when they are infertile, may also be subject to criticism, under some circumstances, for their effects on the participants. So, however, may other human relationships which evoke no such uproar. Jealousy as we understand it is to a large extent a product of social outlook, and of the conception of a partner as personal property, but it has also a number of deep roots in mammalian behaviour, and the cooling of sexual affection is very rarely a simultaneous and bilateral process. While it is possible to modify current attitudes in this field, the idea of 'de-emotionalizing' sex, canvassed at the start of the century, is not one which inspires much enthusiasm, or which enters the field of practical action at the present time.

THE LIMITATION OF COITUS

Institutional marriage cannot, therefore, be attacked for its assertion of the advantages of monogamy. The main defect in the institutional conception lies in the assumptions it makes, in the means it adopts to enforce its assertion, and in its practical failure to secure the desired result. The current form of coercive and institutional marriage, so far from protecting either the child or the partners, penalizes both by attempting to maintain 'for the sake of the children' or in the interest of public morals unions which have never had a reasonable chance of success, in which case the child becomes a missile in the conflict between its parents, or child and aggrieved partner suffer equally from the humiliating accompaniments of legal divorce. To the argument that institutions and sanctions are necessary to restrain would-be delinquents from acting irresponsibly, we are increasingly able to reply that they fail to restrain them, and that there is no substitute for informed public responsibility in personal relationships. Institutional measures such as the tightening up of divorce laws are not, on the evidence, capable of effecting any major change in the pattern of behaviour. In a society that itself creates, by its attitude and its climate, the conditions of failure in marriage, they are as ineffective in bringing about such changes as punishment of the barometer is in modifying the weather.

I have outlined some of the economic and social factors which may interfere with marriage in centralized societies: of these, the consequences of war and militarism, the lack of adequate sexual education, and the effects of asociality on the individual are probably the most important. The current conception of sexual honour has led to a large crop of marriages which fulfill none of the conditions of normality, and are, in fact, transactions at the promiscuous or the adolescent level which masquerade as marriages in the interests of respectability. Our conception of the sexual requirements of the adolescent makes no provision for mate selection, or even for the fact that coital impulses exist long before the individual is emotionally or economically ready for parenthood.

The questions that we need to answer in assisting individuals to find a reasonable basis for their sexual standards are these: What type of relationship is it wisest to aim at? By what steps should it be reached? How far is it advisable that sexual intercourse should be limited to the marital pattern? If marriage is ideally permanent, how can compatibility and security be best assured before parenthood is undertaken? The answer to the first question has been partly given; the answers to the others turn very largely on the significance which the idea of permanent reproductive marriage gives to pre-marital and extra-marital intercourse. Judging by its recurrence in clinical advisory work and in questions to lecturers, especially from young audiences, this question of the limitation of coitus to marriage bulks large in the minds of most people who are in search of a rational sexual ethic.

In a society that had no institutional marriage, all coitus apart from the permanent pattern would be either pre-marital or merely casual. Casual intercourse without any prospect of permanency occurs widely in most cultures – under present social conditions it is deeply involved with the failure of society to provide a stable environment, with war and its effects, and with the consequent replacement of institutional prostitution by the amateur variety. Where it is deliberately chosen as a substitute for a more permanent relationship, it is sometimes a symptom of personal difficulty in adjustment or of low intelligence, and its part in the adaptation and conduct of stable individuals is occasional only. It would have far less social importance than most other signs of emotional difficulties, such as aggression or acquisitiveness, if it did not carry the risk of unwanted pregnancy and of hurting someone. Pre-marital intercourse, on the other hand, is far more obviously a part of the normal process of sexual growth, since its existence as a separate category depends on the point in the love relationship at which institutional marriage comes into effect, and on the centring of marriage in the hymen rather than the uterus. Questioners tend to speak of pre-marital intercourse with two distinct meanings in mind – intercourse between lovers, who are already committed to a permanent relationship at the personal level, and who envisage a stable monogamous union, and coitus prior to marriage on an experimental basis as part of the process of mate selection.[17] In the first case, since the ratification of intercourse by the state is not a landmark in the course of a sexual relationship, the only psychological objections to pre-marital intercourse arise from the attitudes of the partners and of their relatives, and from the anxiety and the complications which result from social disapproval. The argument that he who possesses loves no more is hardly conclusive, because it applies equally to possession under the form of institutional marriage, which has no magic to perpetuate a relationship that never possessed emotional roots going beyond the primary desire for coitus. In the second case, the advisability of promiscuous pre-marital experience has to be weighed against its defects – the unpreparedness of the parties to establish a stable relationship if conception occurs, the risk of venereal disease, and the undesirable character of a home established by accident. All these arguments have been overworked in the past.

A recent study by Kirkendall[28] of the pre-marital adventures of American boys, throws almost as much light on the *naïveté* of humane social investigators as on the behaviour it set out to examine – we read of one young man who, having had pleasurable intercourse with several girls, married a virgin who was frigid: the author's conclusion is that this is an argument against pre-marital coition, for if he had not had it, he might never have known how unsatisfactory his marriage was!

The depressing thing about Kirkendall's young Americans is not their willingness to sleep with school and college friends, or the complete absence of parental supervision or counsel which we sense in the background, but the aggression, egocentricity and general lack of any concern for the girl as a person (boys only were interrogated) which often went with it. This was not limited to the age of sex bravado – older boys seemed to have an equally exploitive attitude, which would prevent them gaining much, or giving anything, in most of these relationships. We may be tempted to see it as a social defect of modern America – or we would be, if the long English ballad tradition did not reflect the same lack of inherent chivalry (one would like to have heard the girls talking equally frankly about their motives, to be fair to all). The main point is, however, that this lack of tenderness or, indeed, of love, would handicap its possessors just as much in marriage as in deriving any maturity

94

from what they did before marriage – and does so handicap a great many adults, nominally chaste or not.

Clearly there is a failure of social education somewhere, If, indeed, we want to talk to the young in terms of sensible moral prohibition (and there is no reason why we should not), then the two most important commandments of this kind now go by default, both here and in America, in the clamour over the importance of physical virginity which has come to replace real moral instruction; these are 'Thou shalt not exploit another person's feelings and wantonly expose them to an experience of rejection' and 'Thou shalt not under any circumstances negligently risk producing an unwanted child.' These are prohibitions which apply quite as much within marriage as outside it. Unlike the injunction of chastity they make sense. They are immediately intelligible and acceptable to any sensible youngster, in precept at least, but since they carry the valid implication that extra-marital coitus which is not exploitive and not negligent is 'all right', the traditionalists prefer, as it were, to keep them in reserve. Hence perhaps the striking lack of both ordinary caution and of chivalry in some youngsters who, having crossed the publicized Rubicon by intromission, stop bothering about any further precept. If so, the fault in such cases could be ours, for teaching rules instead of principles.

The practice of one or both types of pre-marital intercourse is extremely widespread in our own society. In 1938, forty per cent of girls marrying under twenty, thirty per cent marrying at twenty, and twenty per cent marrying at twenty-one were pregnant at the time of marriage, and these figures represent only that proportion of cases in which conception took place. They could probably be doubled to cover all forms of pre-marital experience in coitus.[20] Judging from the age distribution, it looks as though most of the cases belong to the second type, and that the fact of marriage depends rather on the pregnancy than on previous intention. Under these conditions accident and alcohol play a larger part than conscious choice of mate. The chief biological issue is, from our point of view, how far full intercourse among adolescents and young adults is desirable as a method of mate selection. The argument which

PRE-MARITAL SEXUAL INTERCOURSE IN RELATION TO DATE
OF BIRTH (AMERICAN MIXED POPULATION SAMPLE, 1938)*
(PERCENTAGE)

	DATE OF BIRTH			
	Before 1890	1890–99	1900–1909	1910 or later
Husbands				
None	50·6	41·9	32·6	13·6
Spouse only	4·6	7·6	17·2	31·9
Others only	35·6	27·5	16·5	13·6
Spouse and others	9·2	23·0	33·7	40·9
Wives				
None	86·5	74·0	51·2	31·7
Spouse only	8·7	17·7	32·7	45·0
Others only	1·9	2·5	2·1	3·3
Spouse and others	2·9	5·8	14·0	20·0

* Modified from L. M. Terman, *Psychological Factors in
Marital Happiness* (New York: McGraw-Hill, 1938).[20]

recurs among young people is that if we expect monogamy on a
permanent basis it is unrealistic to expect the parties to marry
without some means of assessing sexual function and compatibility. If the stability of marriage depends, in its intention,
on the needs of the child, it is obviously rash to begin it with a
pregnancy and discover incompatibilities later, and it is suggested that these can be avoided by making a trial of cohabita-
tion before accepting any legal obligations. The idea of trial
marriage has had some sociological support and has been tried
in practice under modern urban conditions. In general, it has
not worked conspicuously well. The general conclusion appears to be that adults will obviously regulate their sexual relationships and conduct such trials as they think necessary
according to their circumstances and attitude, and that advice
to them will depend on a knowledge of the parties and of how
exactly they are situated. The problem for adolescents is a good
deal more complex, since the effects of unwanted pregnancy or
unfortunate emotional experiences are, if anything, worse in
this group.

Monogamy and the Pattern of Sexual Conduct

The balance of evidence seems to suggest that ideally older adolescents should be allowed to decide for or against coitus for themselves (which they are doing already in any case), and given the contraceptive facilities on which freedom of choice depends, while younger adolescents are encouraged to 'ca' canny' and progress from play to earnest, as in some of the more permissive tribal societies, by easy stages. The key to realizing this idea is a wholly foolproof form of contraception. We have effective methods now, but perhaps not quite effective enough for us to commit ourselves to advising adolescent intercourse: however, while we are hesitating, adolescent intercourse is already becoming commoner and commoner without benefit of contraceptive education. We might as well, therefore, make up our minds, bearing in mind that within ten years advances in contraceptive technique will probably dispose of ninety-nine per cent of the rational, as opposed to the rationalized, objections to free sexual intercourse at an early age. We may eventually come to realize that chastity is no more a virtue than malnutrition.

The problem of pre-marital conduct is subsidiary to the far larger problem of the desirable age for marriage and the optimal duration of courtship. We are dealing here with a fairly clear-cut divergence of opinion. On one hand, it is recognized that prolonged pre-marital continence has drawbacks outweighing its negative value as an alternative to promiscuity, and that such continence is, and probably always was, largely an academic conception in the light of actual conduct; on the other, evidence is accumulating that marital stability under present conditions is higher after a prolonged courtship, within limits, than when marriage is undertaken on impulse. The increasing psychological overtones of marriage in civilized communities probably demand a longer period of adjustment than the purely physical, and a more gradual process of mate selection is possibly in keeping with the relative slowness of growth into adulthood which often seems to be a characteristic of cultures that reach a high intellectual level. The standard interpretation of morality as something centred in the genitalia has made us commit a monstrous error in amputating the

97

physical expression of sex in adolescence, and the drive towards sensory experiment, from all the other emotional needs of growing up – for independence combined with a sense of support, for competitive status, for reassurance against fears about one's virility or lovability, for reassurance against fear of rejection. In adolescence the two developing streams of physical and emotional experiment should flow towards fusion – by making morals a matter of sexual abstinence only, we actually reinforce their separation – if youngsters never outgrow the attitude which sees the opposite sex as a quarry upon which one chalks up points, the tradition of over-emphasis is largely to blame for their brashness. The drive to experiment usually comes first – communication, mutual affection, a protective attitude to one's partner – love, in fact – comes later.

'TEENAGE MORALS' AND THE CORRUPTION OF THE TIMES

Miss Jo Drury said in her presidential address to the Association of Remand Home Superintendents and Matrons at Bournemouth today:

'Girls we are now getting have no sense of responsibility. They do not know right from wrong and there is only one subject they can talk about, and that is sex. They think that it is part of their lives.'

Mr. Justice Stable, said at Lincs. Assizes, Lincoln, today: 'It is an accepted thing today that these young people seem to attach as much importance to the fact of sexual intercourse as they do to ordering an iced lolly.'

Evening Standard. (Tuesday, October 31, 1961).

'Society, sir, has been so long going to the devil that it is devilish odd it has not yet come there.' Whoever said that (attributions differ) and in whatever age, the occasion was probably the same; for there has been no more popular alarmist activity in any age than the denunciation of modern manners. Usually there is something to denounce: the denouncers have enough of a case to upset well-thinking people, and the act of denunciation meets a deep-seated emotional need in themselves. Moreover, by concentrating on a limited range of abuses – sexual for choice, aesthetic second (now that doctrinal heresy does not convulse us, in the West at least) – such emotive moralists can moralize without the discomfort of having to understand real patterns of social change, and without the risks of attacking more sensitive and less popular targets where power, property, or social privilege are involved.

The young are always the most popular target for this prophetic sniping. They are less experienced than their elders in papering over the differences between real behaviour and professed standards; we, their elders, are expected to advise and chasten them (if we cannot be paternalists to our own children, to whom can we be?); and resentment at their scrapes, their tastes, or their laxness is almost always tinged with our own envy of opportunities which concern us no longer.

But concern at delinquency and real social problems of youth, it may be said, is another matter, too serious to be dismissed like this: we are suggesting that crimes of violence by schoolboys, and syphilis in young girls, are the invention of captious elders? No, but they can be exaggerated; and what characterizes much of the current religio-legal and politico-scholastic attack on the good name of 'teenagers' (the name itself has been coined to steady the aim of the denouncers) is often precisely a lack of such humane concern. Much of it is emotional and ignorant, while some comes painfully close to satisfaction over the supposed ill-effects of moral precept neglected. Many would feel that there is an acid test of humanity in our concern over such matters as venereal disease and illegitimacy: if it is genuine, our first object will be to see that all concerned suffer as little from their mistakes as is humanly possible, rather than to make sure they serve as examples to others, and we shall not regard the spermatozoon and the spirochæte as valuable allies in upholding a morality which, we fear, may prove unable to claim public acceptance without them. We would be the first to resent it if adolescents were to express the hope of seeing us fried by our own atomic bombs if we ignore their warnings against the neglect of other, less popular, Christian injunctions.

Next to the aggression it conceals, the chief feature of much of this criticism of the young is its ignorance. That moral attitudes may be changing is a fair observation, though in all such cases the change in behaviour is probably far less than the change in pretentions. Much of the 'immorality' which convulses the traditionalists is in fact a gain in candour and an increased willingness to speak up for our real standards. It is difficult even for the dispassionate to measure what is changing and how much. Statistics meanwhile are often presented by interested parties who, in the cause of public morals, are quite devoid of shame.

Geoffrey Gorer[30] suggests that the chief important change in custom over the last few decades is that the daughters of the middle class have become mistresses of their persons, and consequently the custodians of their own chastity and behaviour. Having ceased to lock up their daughters, the professional classes have now to face the realities of adolescent sexual needs which the working classes faced for centuries; and they are finding these needs painfully disruptive of the educational stereotype – long schooling, the celibate university, and the advantageous or stable match in the late twenties and early thirties – which this long childhood involves.

The statistics seem to bear this out. They also show that the biggest change in behaviour has been one of timing. The over-all incidence of illegitimate births and of pre-maritally conceived children has remained extremely stable since the 1930s, but in common with all the other statistical indices the distribution has moved to younger age-groups in step with the steady secular fall in the age of physical puberty. Modern youngsters not only develop earlier; they win prizes or prison sentences, go to the ballet, take part in political meetings, and engage in sexual intercourse, earlier. The magnitude of the shift is such that the interests and problems of the sixth-former today are roughly those of the undergraduate yesterday. Some part of this shift may be socially rather than physiologically determined, if only to the extent that slower developers will be carried along by faster: the influence of books, television, and the other war-horses which carry would-be censors to battle, may or may not be real – the point of interest is that it is probably no greater in altering the conduct of this group than that

of their elders. The statistics which show large apparent changes
are almost all ancillary to this age shift: the increase in sexual
offences involving the age of consent is clearly one such figure,
for the age of consent has not advanced with earlier puberty.
The matter is well summarized in the same pamphlet in a few
courageous sentences from the Minister of Education:[30]

> 'The first point is that the morals of teen-agers appear now
> to conform at an earlier age to those of the young adult com-
> munity. . . . A moment or two's reflection should be enough to
> dispose of the notion that there has been any cataclysmal
> change in moral standards between the present generation . . .
> and those immediately before them. In fact, so far as there is a
> "problem" of teen-age morals it is a reflection of the earlier
> physical maturity of young people – their confrontation with
> moral choices at an earlier age.'

The real crisis of teenage morals affects not the teenager but
his elders, who find themselves increasingly defending an ethos
which they are beginning to recognize as unworkable. It is
academic to argue whether youngsters can or even should post-
pone all sexual experience until they can complete their education and set up a professional-class home; for few are doing
so, and still fewer will. It is doubtful, indeed, if their fathers
did so, and today adolescence is earlier and education longer:
for a technologist or a doctor it may now occupy over a
quarter of his expectation of life. We all tend to identify with
the parents or with the children, in such matters. (I tend to
identify with the children, but from this *parti pris* I can make
a case.)

A rationalist would point out that teenagers themselves are
having far less difficulty with the empirical part of this adjustment than their elders, especially those who base their sexual
standards on religious dogmas inaccessible to revision in terms
of reality: while the religious pin their faith, not very hopefully,
on more strenuous argument in defence of what they believe to
be right conduct. The choice of standards which we follow and
which we advocate for our children's guidance is a matter of
personal conviction, and the younger generation will accept or

reject our advice in terms of their own personality, as we accepted or rejected that of our parents. The obligation to let them make such a choice is a difficult one in proportion to the strength of our own convictions. Public morals are in fact changing, and institutions will change with them. Those who from conviction are unable to contemplate any change at all in traditional standards have no obligation to consider how far they are willing to go in resisting the corresponding change in institutions, if that opposition is going to widen the gap between those institutions and real behaviour. Those, for example who conscientiously believe that contraception is an evil must consider seriously whether they ought to force the consequences of that belief on others who disagree with them, by organized clamour against any public instruction in it; in the same way the point is being reached where people who oppose the giving of instruction on contraception and venereal disease to teenagers must consider whether they are not defending a dogma at the expense of human suffering among those who, through 'weakness' or out of actual and no less sincere conviction, ignore the rule they are laying down. It seems reasonable that if contraceptive advice is to be given when it is needed to prevent illegitimate births, and if the age of puberty has advanced far into the school years, then whatever instruction the last generation received at 18, this generation should receive at 15. Adolescent fertility can be dangerously high. Arguments about the undesirability of encouraging sexual experiment have singularly little relation to the modern reality, and are likely to ensure that the most sexually accident-prone minority is the only section of the teenage community which has failed to obtain the requisite information. Those teenagers today who have ordinary initiative can obtain both information and contraceptives; and many use them. The real objection to making such instruction general seems to be the argument that illegitimacy is a valuable safeguard against vice, and should be fostered for the public benefit.

As for our humane concern to spare others unhappiness, there is, unfortunately, only one way of making sure that the mature bodies of our children contain the emotionally mature minds which are needed for the painless management of all personal relations, not only sexual ones; and that is by our own example. Contact with an adult erotic relationship in parents has an educational value which we can easily overlook if we think of all later sexual difficulties in terms of very early psychogenesis; for human beings learn by watching. This does not mean that we should invite our children into the bedroom, as some disturbed people have hinted – but nothing is a better preparation for a happy marriage than to watch the mutual consideration and happiness in their ordinary contacts of two mature people who love each other. Unfortunately, not many adults are mature, and some today are less so in this respect than their children. Irresponsible promiscuity and moralisms based on fear are two polar consequences of such adult immaturity. It ought to be possible for those with insight to ensure that neither of these extremes hold the casting vote in the rearrangement of attitudes to adolescent sexuality which is on its way. The behaviour which these attitudes will accept and guide, or reject and complicate, is already readjusting itself without asking our leave. It would be a gain in frankness and honesty at least, one might think, if in the future the gap between Sunday pretences and weekday reality could be narrowed.

It is unfortunate that so much which is written about early sex experience and teenage behaviour is written by men and by unmarried women – for perhaps the key problem of sex education, physical, social and moral, is to give boys, who in our culture are the more sexually aggressive, some rudimentary insight into the way in which girls' responses differ from their own. For a man, defloration is an achievement but no more – if anything, he is doing his partner a favour making a woman of her. For the girl, every act of penetration, then or later, is an invasion of her body by forces outside herself. She can never feel exactly the same towards a man who has 'known' her thus, even if only once – many boys are staggered by the change in her attitude which one act of intercourse can bring about, and her intensity may scare them off. Women are neither biologically nor intellectually 'weaker vessels', and neither sex should be brought up

103

with such illusions, but they are, in our culture, much more vulnerable to a sense of rejection – this can be as traumatic to them as denigration of his virility to a boy, and its effects can be as lasting.

But at the same time, these hazards to ourselves and to others are a part of human life, and attend every human relationship. If we gave overmuch thought to the risk we run of injury and of injuring we should never dare to love or marry, but aim, like the Lord Buddha, to suppress all emotion and desire 'since by these suffering comes', and frighten our young into doing the same. Such counsels come in real life from women who have had bitter experiences, and thereby set their daughters to distrust men and repress their response to them; and from men who have suffered from demanding, unhappy wives and teach their sons to be scared of feminine hysteria and emotional blackmail: '*Moi*,' says an Anouilh father, '*j'filais toujours le premier* . . .' This kind of grudge is self-propagating. Much as we want to spare our children our own mistakes, it is criminal to make them unduly nervous or teach them to reject experience. Unless we do, they will fall in love, they will experiment with their bodies and with their emotions, and they cannot help leaning upon one another, a process which produces, like climbing or walking in infancy, some bruises and even an occasional fatality. If we make sure that we disapprove, cannot be talked to, and have to be deceived, by putting an explicit or implicit ban on sexual experiment, we probably only succeed in sharply augmenting the casualty rate. Physically hardy and active men and women do not try to frighten their sons and daughters out of the sports, achievements and dangers they have experienced themselves – only to train them not to be duffers or take and inflict foolish risks through inexperience – knowing that they probably will and must take some in the course of learning, but that the rewards of physical activity fully justify the dangers. The same is true of emotional activity – love in its various manifestations is, after all, the justification for living at all, and gives us all our most rewarding, as well as some of our bitterest, moments. It will do the same, if we are wise, for our children.

SEXUAL EQUIVALENTS IN MATE SELECT*

Primitive societies deal with the same prob.
ways. In many, emotional maturity is reached earn....
marriage on a permanent basis can occur at an early age. In
a few, the pattern of society permits adolescent coitus, and
there is evidence to suggest that in some cases a physiological
infertility exists during the period of mate selection. Others
adopt a number of tolerated sexual equivalents as a substitute
for coitus. Equivalents of this kind are the means by which the
majority of adolescents in British and American society conduct their first courtship experiments. They are, of course,
neither new nor always clandestine. The Welsh 'courting on the
bed' or the New England custom of 'bundling' represent forms
of adolescent and early adult sexual outlet that are common in
peasant cultures. Adolescents adopt them naturally in most
cultures where they are restrained from full coitus by social or
moral considerations.

Among the African Bhaca, for example, 'children early
become acquainted with the facts of sex. One of the first games
played is called *indize* (hide and seek): opportunity is frequently
taken on these occasions for sexual play between boy and girl.
After about the age of eight young boys and girls meet on
moonlit nights for singing and dancing, afterwards pairing off
and sleeping together: parents know about this but do not
mind "so long as the children are happy"'. This intimacy is
continued into adolescence – the technique which is then permitted is called *tshina* or *metsha* – intercrural intercourse without penetration. This is 'a socially approved custom, and young
people at puberty are instructed in its techniques, the mothers
of young girls in particular stressing the dangers of uncon-
trolled sexual intercourse'. Pregnancy is considered a disgrace –
but the modern Bhaca youngster is less patient than formerly.
'The technique seems to have been for the girl to draw her
beadwork apron between her legs, but today this method seems
to be falling into disuse. From investigations among school
people it appears that full intercourse is taking the place of the
traditional method, with a consequent increase in illegitimate

105

births.'[31] One could cite many comparable examples in other peoples. In Dahomey the view appears to be that children should be encouraged in prepubertal sexual experiment but not given exact details of adult intercourse, for 'if they knew how, they would do it.'[32]

In Wogeo (New Guinea) the official teaching is that coition is bad for boys, and stunts their growth, but this, according to one of the younger generation, is 'a tale of the old men to keep us quiet;' they know women prefer our smooth skin and straight limbs.'[33]

Equivalent forms of sexual stimulation vary from manual "groping" to abortive forms of intercourse with a 'wide range of genital and somatic contacts. There is a good deal of evidence that sub-sexual experience of this kind plays a considerable part in helping to bridge the gap between childhood and adulthood, and they are typical of the selection period, in which emotions are still labile and the readiness for a permanent choice has not yet developed. They also play a part in the sexuality of older persons when other outlets are not available. The equivalents practised in Western countries have not been studied in detail, but they most commonly take the form of manual stimulation, so-called 'clothed intercourse' (genital stimulation by body friction, the parties being clothed), and more rarely other techniques. American adolescents, who appear to have systematized pre-courtship to a striking degree, distinguish between various categories of 'light' and 'heavy' petting, which cover most of the forms of courtship behaviour short of penetration.

The arguments levelled against behaviour of this type fall into two groups – a physiological and a moralistic, the first serving very often as substitutes for the second. Some writers have suggested that stimulation short of intercourse is in itself a factor in producing anxiety states and in preventing the formation of adult sexual response. It is increasingly clear however, that very few sexual activities produce ill effects on mental health, apart from those which arise from conflict with the standards of the subject or those of his home and society. It is reasonable to assume that most of the psychological ill effects of sexual equivalents, if shown to exist at all, result from the concealment and lack of toleration that attend it. It has been repeatedly stated that long-continued stimulation without penetration tends to establish a conditioning to external genital contacts and to hinder the establishment of vaginal orgasm. It is very doubtful whether such a mechanism really exists, however, and no convincing physiological evidence for it has been put forward. Kinsey's[14] figures for an American college population contradict the assumption. 'There is . . . considerable evidence that pre-marital petting contributes definitely to the effectiveness of sexual relations after marriage.' Terman's[20], on the other hand, show a slight balance against 'petting' among successfully married couples. This, however, was carried on by adolescents who were really old enough for full intercourse rather than the younger age-groups making their earliest sex contacts. It may well be that the determining factor is the attitude of the experimenters, their parents, and their teachers, rather than anything in the experiments themselves. A distinction can also be drawn between 'stable marriage' and 'effective sexual relations'. It seems reasonable to regard the progress of sexual experience from childhood to maturity as lying through solitary self-stimulation, sexual play, and permanent choice of a partner to full intercourse on a reproductive basis.

Most informed non-Catholics now recognize adolescent masturbation as a normal and harmless manifestation, and have ceased to frighten schoolboys with threats of insanity, blindness and pimples resulting from it, but even the most enlightened tend to spoil the demonstration by equivocal warnings about excess and self-control which, though well-intended, tend to sow doubts. 'Excess' in sexual performance is a meaningless term – in one sense it is impossible, because there is a physiological limit on performance. The potential sexual performance of young adolescents is, in terms of number of orgasms, very high indeed, but even a marathon of this kind produces no greater fatigue than any other athletic feat, and less than most. The widespread belief propagated by sports masters that loss of semen is itself exhausting, draining the virility and causing – in

the words of a recent French pseudo medical book – a 'ruinous
loss of phosphates' is plain unvarnished superstition. The fact
that the volume and solids of the ejaculate fall steadily with
repetition should make this evident even if, like the Tantrik
Buddhists, we invest the easily-replaced nucleic acids of the
spermatozoa with magic properties. There would in fact be
some reason to expect that frequent early masturbation might
provide valuable training for later married life by lowering the
sensitivity of the penis and prolonging the interval before
orgasm: strenuous abstinence is, in practice, a common pre-
cursor of premature ejaculation (though we would not now go
along with the advice of Fallopius, 'to work hard to enlarge the
child's member while still an infant, for a well-grown yard never
comes amiss' – *Ego moneo parentes ut studeant in aetate infantili
ut magnificetur membrum puerorum: magnum etenim nun-
quam inutile est* – irritants and massage being the recommended
means!) There is at least no evidence that frequent orgasm
obtained in this fashion is in any way harmful, provided that
there is no adult-fostered guilt or anxiety attached to it.[67] It
seems an important aim of sex education to see that there is not,
and that the boy's or the girl's first encounter with sex in this
form shall be frankly pleasurable, not merely tolerated. It
might, indeed, be wise for the parents themselves to forestall
other less permissive instruction by telling their children: 'You
will soon find, if you haven't already, that you can get a special
kind of pleasure from rubbing the genitalia, and that you need
to do this fairly often. This is a kind of rehearsal for the grown-
up sex act, and perfectly good and natural – but keep quiet
about it, and don't be upset if you encounter adults who tell you
that it is diseased, sinful and so on: they all did the same at the
same age.'

The early adolescent equivalents in general use between
couples are probably equally beneficial to the process of growth,
provided they are not accompanied by guilt and conflict, or
continued far into adult life without normal progress to maturer
relationships, and provided that mutual orgasm is secured.
Failure to achieve satisfaction does certainly result in anxiety,
and in a great heightening of the emotional tension; un-

satisfactory or ignorant attempts, therefore, are more likely to prove harmful, and, incidentally, to provoke excursions into full coitus before the partners are ready for it.

It is the fear of this added excitement which underlies much of the moralistic criticism of sexual equivalents. We must rush to substitute cold baths, mountain climbing, and what Kurt Hahn revealingly calls the 'non-poisonous emotions'. Apart from this, the main argument, when it is not a rationalization of other attitudes, and of a fundamental hostility towards all sexual experience, is that adolescent 'petting' is an incitement to coitus and that the parties are 'playing with fire.'[26] As far as England is concerned, this argument must wait for accurate data, but Kinsey's figures, based on American adolescents, suggest that in those groups where love-play short of intercourse is common, the incidence of pre-marital coitus is abnormally low, and proportionately high in social groups which reject petting as unnatural. Moreover, unsympathetic adult attitudes towards adolescent sexual experiment ensure that it will be clandestine, that it will frequently be ill informed, and even that it will be regarded as morally equivalent to fornication – this last view is less prevalent than formerly among parents, but it might well lead intelligent youngsters to prefer hanging for a sheep to hanging for a lamb. For many of them, in present conditions, coitus *will* probably follow within a few years, and the fact should be accepted and allowed for.

Opinion among sexual educators already favours a sensible and helpful attitude to adolescent sexuality rather than a shocked attempt at restriction, and it already accepts the need for giving factual information; it is considerably less willing to commit itself to any positive encouragement for adolescent sexual equivalents. As with masturbation in younger children, the tendency is to give sympathetic reassurance to those who are anxious, coupled with the counsel to abstain so far as possible. This view, however, has defects. Any advocacy of sexual practice, given under cover of sex instruction, would make many parents and educators retire in disorder. The logic of such a retreat is inadequate. The very fact of giving sexual instruction lays on the educators a duty to assist the child with something more concrete than warnings. By withholding definite and suitable outlets other than those the child can discover for himself, we leave open a far wider gap for enterprises which may go badly wrong.

It seems that the solution most in accordance with modern knowledge lies in an intelligent giving of advice to young adolescents, through the parents and through the ordinary channels of sex education, about the forms of sexual play that are most likely to lead to orgasm for both parties, and least likely to result in conception or an undesirable carry-over into adult practice, coupled with a definite social tolerance of such equivalents as will enable them to be open and not clandestine, and with the full recognition that they will later, in some at least, be replaced by coitus. There is, of course, no suggestion that the classroom, or that stand-by of sex-educators, the biology syllabus, provided a venue for this type of teaching, any more than for other education in social behaviour. Even allowing for the normal reticence of adolescents, the intelligent parent or teacher can safely be left to discover proper openings. 'Special parades' in any field of sex education probably do more harm than good.[34] Nor should teaching of this kind be allowed to devolve on the embarrassed or on tactless enthusiasts. The older method of prohibition, and the newer of giving some theoretical but no practical counsel, both hamper adjustment and encourage 'trouble' of the kind they aim to avoid. We can regulate these experiments, or help the participants to regulate them, only if we cease to insure that they occur under unfavourable circumstances and without intelligent advice. The prohibitive outlook carries the implicit suggestion that marriage should be undertaken without experience of anything but solitary, and therefore unregulated, stimulation. Those to whom the prospect is alarming should realize, therefore, that in giving this advice we are not creating a new pattern of behaviour – adolescent sexual experience is, and will remain, widespread; by withholding advice we shall not prevent it, but we shall forfeit the opportunity of insuring that it is beneficial.

This type of instruction involves several prerequisites. It is essential to make sure that the adolescent audience has a perfectly clear idea of the circumstances in which conception may take place – one still meets bizarre superstitions derived from adults and other adolescents, and fears of pregnancy in young girls who have been kissed or have danced with a man – ignorance in either direction is almost equally dangerous. It is also important to stress the reasons why coitus is undesirable just yet rather than codes of 'clean living' or virginity, or rationalized versions of such codes. The answer to the growing problem of adolescent promiscuity, which is undesirable on some counts, lies in the inculcation of an early and intelligent understanding of the reasons why the family must be considered as a permanent unit, coupled with sympathetic advice and toleration for equivalents, and the encouragement of early marriage when, and not before, adult judgment and development have been reached. We persistently underrate the rationality of adolescents – in many ways it is less liable to rationalized evasions than the standards of adults. The child who has learned that the infant requires a stable environment *in utero* can equally well understand why it requires a similar parental stability. Standards stated on reasonable grounds are generally acceptable to the young, while unsubstantiated preaching is regarded as impertinent and insincere. Tolerated equivalents are in themselves an introduction to the finer and more mature conception of sexuality, and to the need for mutual accommodation and respect. In this sense they probably contribute to the pattern of sex education something which cannot be verbally taught and help the adolescent to outgrow the narcissistic attitude of the earlier phases of development, which jeopardizes many marriages and makes many insufferable partners by its persistence into adult life.

'Petting' among American adolescents is regulated, like much other social conduct in the same age group, by a rigid system of group opinion, and, like other adolescent activities, it appears to be taken inordinately seriously by the participants. Where toleration prevents it from being wholly solitary, the body of 'good form' is in itself an insurance of sensible behaviour – the 'wolf' and the irresponsible incur the disapproval which they unfortunately fail to meet in adult society. Instruction in sex equivalents, then, is clearly to be confined to a suitable age group, and given informally. The audience can be encouraged to regard such knowledge as the privilege of age, not to be distributed indiscriminately to younger children who are not ready for it. It seems that by forbidding the very young intercourse on what still at the moment seem good grounds, and withholding alternatives on bad, we run the risk of losing a particularly valuable means of social and personal education, and of destroying the whole logic of sex-hygiene teaching. Knowledge without the chance to use it is more a source of tantalization than of development. It seems reasonable to suggest that while the child learns about the physical and biological aspects of sexuality, he should also learn something about its impact on others and himself, first by learning to manipulate his own body, and later by sharing his experiments with others, always with the knowledge that it is a means towards fuller and more adult patterns of privilege and responsibility to which he can intelligently look forward.

EARLY MATURITY

'At the age of twelve years he was a married man, And at the age of thirteen years the father of a son – But before his fourteenth year was up, his grave was grassy green; Cruel Death had put an end to his growing.'

Over the last century the age of puberty in both sexes has been advancing steadily by about five months per decade. In girls, where there is a simple point of reference, the average age of first menstruation has fallen from about 17 years in 1850 to 13.7 years in 1950. The trend in boys appears to be comparable.[53]

This increase in the rate of child development seems to be general in the socially-privileged countries. The main cause of it is almost certainly better feeding and hygiene; the abandonment of habitual over-clothing and under-exercise may also have contributed. These causes seem sufficient in themselves, though socio-genetic mechanisms have also been invoked. With earlier puberty, all the indices of physical maturity, and some of the indices of social and intellectual maturity, appear to have advanced also. A change of this sort, though gradual, may be expected to have practical implications going beyond increasing the difficulty of recruiting choirboys of amenable age. At the moment we do not know how long the trend can be expected to continue, or what consequences we should expect from it in other than physical fields, but it is obviously desirable to foresee such consequences if possible.

Juvenile 'precocity' is a subject which by its nature ensures that comment will not wait for facts, even though the kind of precocity which attracts such comment is probably more often cultural than physiological in origin. Before 'unnatural' precocity joins the decay of moral standards as a subject for magisterial dicta, it ought to be pointed out that the trend to earlier development – so far at least – seems to represent only a return to normal after a period in the late 18th and early 19th century when puberty was abnormally delayed. Roman Law, the Abbé Brantome, and old medical writers agree in putting the usual age of first menstruation between $12\frac{1}{2}$ and 14 years. In publishing the ballad of the 'Bonny Boy', Baring Gould changed the age of the untimely marriage to 16 years in deference to Victorian taste. Another longstanding conviction which is still with us – that precocity, especially sexual precocity, must be 'paid for' in short life – needs more study, but its appearance in the ballad should warn us against being prejudiced by folk-lore.

In point of fact a far more practically important matter than the average increase in developmental rate, and one which gives rise to far more problems, is the size of the scatter now present in individual growth-patterns. Since potentially rapid developers are now realizing their potentialities, we are now seeing the full extent of this genetic and epidenetic scatter. Not only are some children still children at ages when others are physically mature men and women, but since the development of intelligence is linked with the timing of pubertal growth, the timing of scholastic and social development in individuals who will ultimately be of similar intelligence is equally variable. This can greatly affect their careers, and, since our culture places large premiums on early development, their personality as well. Rate-determining factors seem to account for more and more of the differences between individuals (it is a fascinating speculation whether the difference between neurotic and normal development in Freudian terms is of this kind, making the persistence of childhood anxieties comparable to short sight or persistence of the thymus gland[9,11,12]). Meanwhile a boy who can muster the mental age of twelve at the real age of ten will 'have the edge' on his rivals. He may not be able to keep it up, but by the time they overtake him, he will have secured a privileged place, and that, so far as he is concerned, is what matters.[56] Predictions, prescriptions and syllabi based on the *average* rate of development have therefore the same drawbacks as hats of *average* size (the modal rate would be preferable); moreover in any two children, even the physical marks of puberty may not appear in the same sequence, and these are less subject to the additional, social, influence which can affect subtler forms of maturation.

Although it would not help us to deal with this diversity, the simplest case from the point of view of organization would be that in which intelligence, social experience, sexual behaviour and physical development all, on the average, tended to advance in step – all the other relevant statistical measures should then move with the age of puberty. Some apparently do so. It has been shown that as early as $6\frac{1}{2}$ children who are physically ahead of their age-mates score higher in tests. Both testable intelligence and the appearance of 'adult' interests undergo a sharp spurt at the time of the pubertal growth-wave. 'Maturity', by contrast – in the value-sense implied when we discuss 'readiness' to marry or to comprehend Greek tragedy, rather than to wear long trousers or shave – is not biologically testable: unlike physical puberty, there are many adults who manifestly never reach it. Whether early development has led to 'maturity' of behaviour at a younger age is accordingly a matter of opinion – what does seem likely is that the eventual adult pattern seen in the past is simply being reached earlier; it looks as if this were true both of delinquency (children who would once have been in trouble at sixteen are now in trouble at fourteen) and of positive activities and interests. Audiences at concerts and the ballet, political marchers, discussion group members, all look younger than ever, as if characteristic undergraduate interests had moved into the Sixth Form. It is easy to think of social reasons for this kind of change – they may well represent earlier opportunity and greater sophistication rather than physical precocity. It is also not impossible that the two forces, social and physical, reinforce each other, and that earlier opportunity and sophistication themselves have physical effects.

In the field which generates most of the affect behind public comment on early development, in ballads or on Benches, this is certainly so; sociosexual 'age' has a large physical component, but it is also culture-determined. Little girls in the United States who begin 'dating' at nine are propelled not by hormones but by imitation of older sisters and friends, who are themselves imitating others still older. In some societies as we have seen, child play merges easily and continuously with pre-marital and adult sexual activity. Overt sexual activity in boys generally appears sharply at puberty, but the culture determines what form it is able to take. (The comparable female index is pregnancy; this can be prevented culturally from advancing with earlier ovulation, but cannot advance unless ovulation occurs earlier.)

If in sexual matters adolescents are particularly hard hit by the difference between 'overt' and 'real' mores (in plain, between what we say and what we do), the large differences of development between individuals of the same age is a further complication. Our society at least shows no tendency to slow down the appearance of sociosexual interest, but sternly rejects its expression; our institutions and educational system assume that this rejection is, and will be, observed, an assumption which is sanguine to the point of unreality, though so far as middle-class youngsters are concerned, we have until recently been fairly successful in seeing that sex is not expressed heterosexually. At the same time, while physical maturity has been getting earlier, the period of economic dependence continues to get longer and longer. Childhood and higher education can occupy just under a third of the average life span. Discussions of early marriage must reckon with this, as well as with the fact that one thing which precocity cannot hasten is the acquisition of life-experience – there is also something to be said for childhood itself. Maidenhood, to quote another ballad, is not only a 'heavy burden' of which one is well rid in favour of domestic and sexual responsibilities.

EXTRA-MARITAL RELATIONS

Quite another aspect of the relationship between coitus and marriage is raised when we come to discuss the significance of fidelity. The prevalent conception of marriage, both in the law and in the religious code, insists that any act of sexual intercourse by either party with a third is ground for censure – in the eyes of the law it is also ground for ending the marriage. Without overrating the human desire for variety, which is at least partially counterpoised by a desire for stability, it seems clear that this view is not essentially a part of monogamy, and if we accept reproductive monogamy as a standard, we must base our judgements on the significance of fidelity on its effects on the stability of the home. It is obvious that 'adultery' does in fact frequently upset domestic relations, but a very large part of the damage to the mutual respect of the parties arises from the attitude of society and of individuals. It is probably less true to say that adultery causes the break-up of homes than that it is frequently a deliberate cutting of the link between parties in a home which has already been destroyed by other causes. Its prevalence in wartime is a consequence of forms of separation which leave no outlet for the people separated. Under the circumstances of military service, the probability that intercourse will take place outside marriage depends on the personalities and standards of the husband and wife. Men who have no moral or aesthetic objections to intercourse with prostitutes figure less often in the divorce courts than those who have, because their lapses are usually undetected; it is probably the more sensitive types, who cannot accept a wholly physical estimate of coitus, who get into the most trouble, by incurring new responsibilities and by establishing a positive emotional relationship with their mistresses. Even a more Spartan self-control may jeopardize the marriage, by leading to a projection of resentment against the absent wife; real or imaginary failings in an idealized lover are underlined by the self-approval which comes from several years of strenuous fidelity. In the woman, who has both the consequences of pregnancy and those of a dual system of public morality on her mind, the choice has tended to lie between an acceptance of the repercussions of infidelity and a continent anxiety state.

It has been said that men, as opposed to women, are polyerotic as well as monogamous, but differences in male and female attitude are largely a social phenomenon rather than an unalterable human character, and the same applies to what we may term the 'possessive' concept of fidelity – that a species of property exists in the sexual partner. Very many men, and women, are sincerely capable of loving two people at once, and without unfavourable comparisons between them. It seems very unlikely that 'fidelity', even in its accepted sense, and allowing for idiosyncrasy, would present difficulties to a pair of well-matched and stable personalities who were genuinely in love and not subject to external separating forces. But it is obvious that the capacity of individuals for such stability, or for continence in prolonged separation, differs very widely with personality and circumstance. There is no imaginable reason why a measure of extra-marital intercourse, whether it arises under stress or as an assertion of independence, should necessarily break up the monogamous pattern; even in a society that holds the attitude of our own, this rupture does not occur naturally. Frequently it is brought about by pressure from friends and relatives who urge divorce as a social duty.

A very important factor in altering the pattern of monogamy, and sexual life generally, in our society is the change in attitude towards what used to be called 'middle age'. The years after forty were traditionally viewed by our predecessors as a plateau sloping gradually towards old age, and a time for enjoying what one had, detaching oneself from sexuality and preparing to die content, while deliberately avoiding new experiences in order to facilitate the process. The emotional complications, divorces, and love affairs which have always notoriously characterized this age were regarded as evidence of exceptional instability. This stereotype has been fairly thoroughly shattered in our culture, and the years of former incipient stability (or resignation) are now increasingly recognized as a second adolescence leading to a 'second chance'. We no longer cease to be competitive at 40. Men and women who have raised one family in a marriage which partially satisfied their unconscious and conscious needs have come to realize that they are still free to make a second attempt – although in practice the same unconscious compulsions often make them repeat identical mistakes in partner-selection or in attitude.

The legend of rapidly declining sexual desire has also been discredited by survey studies – in women, up to the age of at least 60, libido commonly goes on increasing, especially with the removal of the fear of conception; in men there is some decline in the 'outlet' – as the number of copulations per week is now inelegantly called – but the average age of ceasing regular coitus is about 68 in married and 58 in unmarried men (in Holland)[35], while 70 per cent of modern American couples were still having frequent orgasm at 60, and many continued into their 80's, the record ages for regular coitus with mutual orgasm in Kinsey's series being over 90.

It is odd that this role of the climacteric, as a second adolescence rather than the antechamber to the grave, which Jung among psychologists was almost alone in noting, has never been fully recognized in our cultural stereotype of monogamy, or in our culture generally. Others have been more flexible, and have recognized and admitted that the fifth decade is a normal period of sexual experimentation, even for happily-married people, in which, with the restraints of child-rearing removed, sexuality acquires a more wholly erotic and fantasy-fulfilling significance than in young fertile marriages. As in the teenage period of adolescence, some people react to the mixture of physiological and life-situation changes by illness or break-down – others launch into new sexual relationships supplementary to, or replacing, what they already have. This can be

more than an insightless attempt to 'regain one's youth' by
pursuing younger lovers – often the new object of affection is
not younger, only different – and much of the strife incidental
to the process is culture-manufactured, through the belief that
one cannot sincerely love two people at once. French society
has long known better, and quite undeservedly became for our
ancestors an emblem of lascivious sophistication in consequence – a miscalculation we are now correcting. A culture which
prepares itself for a new instalment of life at 40, rather than for
the bath-chair and the grave, to which, on existing vital
statistics, it is barely half-way, needs to make some gesture of
recognition towards the change which this implies – we now
have two sex lives, which may be continuous or distinct, and
give wider opportunities, both for fulfilment and for making
ourselves and others miserable, than the simpler and more
compulsive one-shot life-history which used to be the norm.

There is thus a definite tendency for married people, even
when they have strong ties to their partner, to become involved
in sexual exploits outside marriage after it has lasted for some
years. The wife in any culture can hardly fail to be wounded,
and deeply wounded, by a dereliction that implies, in her view,
the decline of her own beauty and vitality, or the husband by
the long tradition of mockery directed at 'cuckolds': but resentment and divorce are not appropriate responses, even if
they are comprehensible ones. One task of marriage guidance is
to prevent the belligerent advice of relatives from increasing
the mischief.

There can be few couples who do not experience strain over
one another's foibles, and fewer still who do not, if they are
quite honest, sometimes desire a sexual holiday: the personal
tensions involved are as painful as all such crises must be, but
when they have been released, the marriage, even if it is childless, or its children grown up, may regain a deeper level of
stability than before. It is highly probable that adultery today
maintains far more marriages than it destroys. Unfulfilled life-
aims in men seem to be more easily exorcised in such a way than
the tensions a woman experiences in the same circumstances,
and for a woman the emotional consequences of rejection seem

to be more serious. The duality of response in man and woman in our culture at least, is real, although the duality of ethical standards is clearly indefensible. The first step to appeasement is for them to recognize each other as people whose needs are intelligible and perfectly worthy.

From the standpoint of advice, we can deal with problems of 'infidelity' in many ways – by trying to dissipate the idea of obligatory divorce, and of adultery as a personal injury, by increasing respect for the personal freedom of the parties, by emphasizing the importance of understanding needs rather than demanding rights, and, above all, by trying to insure that specific situations of this kind are considered at the same level as other personal problems, and not a higher emotional rate of exchange. 'Infidelity' during the period of child growth is likely to have undesirable effects, but where it occurs there too the damage is proportional to the emotional uproar that attends it. If we can induce husbands and wives to regard one another as human beings whose conduct is comprehensible, and remove what may be called the operatic aspect of marriage, we can do a great deal to reduce emotional difficulties of this kind to the level of other personal problems. Jealousy is clearly compatible, up to a point, with radical mutual respect, and no amount of psychology will draw the teeth of the emotional problems that are always involved in the social intercourse of two people over a long period; but there are signs that, left alone by society, the parties can and will settle their difficulties more easily than when they are subject to social and moral pressure. 'Incontinence' is not so serious a social evil as incomprehension, as can be seen in the implacable attitude of continent husbands returning to lonely and less successfully continent wives, where the feeling of virtue unrewarded plays a large part in preventing a sensible solution. The apology —

> If ever any beauty I did see
> Which I desir'd and got, 'twas but a dream of thee—

contains a greater element of truth than some aggrieved parties might willingly admit.

As most people today still believe that love is a fixed quantity, and that love of one person makes impossible love of two or more, the average man or woman falling in love with someone else switches over every atom of sexual emotion to the new person.[38]

This is a misconception that heightens the distress or resentment of the person who feels himself or herself deserted. It is also one which has profoundly affected our interpretations of fidelity. Situations arise within marriage which, without any prejudice to the basic idea of the monogamous unit, are best solved by intercourse outside marriage, and if individuals can make this kind of adjustment we need not interfere, but they raise problems in connection with the third party; in other words, like all sex adjustments they must be made to measure.

To this same field of special cases belong the problems raised in our society by the 'excess' of women over men. It is extraordinarily difficult to offer any constructive answer to the difficulties experienced by this 'surplus'. (It will in any case be short-lasting, for more men than women are conceived, and steady reduction of male mortality is already tending to a male surplus, which may prove in the end even more intractable.) A minority, rather larger than that among males, is able to dispense both with sexual experience and with its social accompaniments. Another minority could be fully satisfied by a limited experience of physical intercourse. But for the majority of unmarried women, neither casual relationships nor substitutes such as masturbation can be regarded as even approaching adequacy. Nothing can replace love -- certainly not 'sex' without it. The social and personal connotations of sexual partnership are equal if not superior in importance to the physical, and the restriction of scope that women still experience in many fields aggravates the difficulty of adjustment. In general, expedients which have been suggested cater to the physical need rather than the emotional. Some such women feel that childbirth and the upbringing of a child would fill some part of the gap, but the advisability of this pattern from the child's point of view is doubtful. We cannot prescribe a child as we could a pill – few children react well to becoming the undivided focus of parental emotions. Sublimation of sexual and emotional needs in social

121

or religious activity, a standard remedy, results in consequences
that are often pathological and bring very little demonstrable
benefit to the patient or to the cause or religion she embraces.
While physical expedients may help some people, and intensive
physical or mental activity may prevent others from stagnating,
the question put by the unmarried and unmarriageable woman
is not one we can settle in general terms. One can give a good
deal of psychological help to individuals, but only if the personality and the circumstances of the subject are known. It will
always be difficult to prevent a sense of inferiority from developing in those who are sexually and socially unsuccessful, and we
are dealing with a primary emotional problem rather than a
matter of sexual ethics. It has been suggested that the difficulty
experienced by many women in adopting an aggressive attitude
towards sexuality, and the tradition that makes the woman the
recipient of a male proposal, have some biological foundation,
in that the female, being evolutionarily the older unit in reproduction, has developed less far in sexuality than the male, and
can dissipate a greater proportion of her energies in fields of
reproductive and social behaviour that are not directly associated with orgasm. This theory is in no sense an excuse for reducing the role of physical satisfaction in the life of the average
woman, but it might account for the failure of purely physical
experiences to satisfy all women as readily as they appear to
satisfy most men. Every woman who fails to find a permanent
sexual and social partner is likely to present, in any society, a
psychiatric problem of varying complexity, and modern knowledge does not suggest that her difficulties can be solved at a
cheap rate by any single change in accepted patterns of conduct.
In most cases our attempted answers are likely to fall very short
of the desirable pattern of sexual relationships, though we can
probably do more than previous generations to deal with
individual difficulties as they arise.

CONTINENCE AND SOCIETY

In adopting an attitude to monogamy based upon any statement of a general principle of mental hygiene and upon recogni-

tion of a wide range of individual attempts at adaptation, we have to reckon with one other criticism, to which I made a passing reference in an earlier section. A number of workers have followed Unwin[37] in his assertion, based on convincing study of primitive cultures, that the intellectual vitality of a culture can be shown to be proportional to the restrictions it imposes upon the basically amorphous sexual freedom of extremely unsophisticated races. Unwin's general conclusion led him to state that 'any society in which pre-nuptial sexual freedom has been permitted for at least three generations will be in the zoistic condition,' this condition representing the most primitive and least inherently civilized form of religious and social pattern, and that which displays the lowest capacity for spontaneous development into a higher pattern.

This view, based originally on anthropology would now find very few anthropological supporters, though it might have had the approbation of Freud, judging from his *Civilization and its Discontents*. It has been received with great favour by those who saw in it a strong argument for the institutional pattern of morals. Mace,[38] for example, contends that it 'gives scientific validity to a fact which has always been tacitly recognized — that the relaxation of sexual restraints has invariably led to the downfall of a civilization.' This historically quite unsupported view follows from a singular conception of sublimation as a means of generating psychical energy, similar to the damming up of water in order to generate hydro-electric power (the analogy is Mace's).

We might possibly, on psychological grounds expect evidence of the transference of energy by sexual repression in some aim-inhibited individuals. Kinsey found no evidence in the private lives of artists that they were converting their sexual energies into art-making; but there are a good many examples of frustration producing a flood of creative works which ceased again when the frustration itself was removed. Still, however the total attitude of a community towards sexual institutions may modify its capacity for progress, there is no evidence whatever to suggest that the individual can look to prolonged physical abstinence for any added reserves of psychic energy. To some extent the tensions of abstinence, or of ungratified desire, may be productively reflected in art, a night of love, in Balzac's words, being another book unwritten – in many artists the reverse is true – but there is no positive correlation in modern statistical research between continence and capacity for work, or between abstinence and heightened nonsexual activity.

> Sublimation is . . . the most inappropriate remedy to offer to a society already suffering from discouragement and frustration. . . . The truth is, as we can convince ourselves by studying history, that sublimation is possible only for individuals and societies that are *not* frustrated.[39]

It would be easy to argue that pre-nuptial abstinence bears a relationship, in civilized societies, to the growth of a responsible attitude towards parenthood, but it is extremely doubtful whether the conscious arguments for the restriction of intercourse which we have discussed play any part in the forming of historical attitudes, and they are certainly absent from primitive cultures. The anxiety of some writers to extend Unwin's idea, which is probably wrong in any case, from its original context of pre-marital continence to the intrinsic value of suppressing sexual experience is only too readily comprehensible. We should not be justified in basing an attempt to ascertain and support a system of responsible sexual behaviour upon any supposed merit present in abstention, or upon any benefit that can be derived from it, because there is no evidence of such benefit, while evidence of the tensions and pathological processes resulting from an enforced and unwilling abstinence are fairly distinctly indentifiable. 'Abstinence' has assumed its present proportions as a problem of sexual study only because it has been so strenuously upheld as a positive virtue. It is probably rather rare. The real problems are almost wholly problems of pattern selection and of social regulation. The 'accepted Christian standard' of sexual behaviour is now seen to be biologically speaking quite unrealistic, and there is no reason to suppose that it has ever represented the practice of more than a minority. We cannot reasonably adopt a standard which assumes either the capacity for abstinence of any major section of the population, or the possibility of excluding individuals from sexual activity compatible with their personality, unless the results of admitting such activity are gravely prejudicial to others. Sexual experience is a normal part of normal living; it can be regulated, by the standards or the reason of the individual, but the wish to exclude it is itself pathological.

The case for pre-marital continence, such as it is, and rationalisations apart, rests on *ad hoc* arguments, not on any general deduction from anthropology. It depends almost wholly on the risk of conception. Advances in contraceptive knowledge may at any moment nullify what is left of this case by removing the possibility of accidental conception altogether; our standards would then have to be formulated in terms of effects on the participants, and it is doubtful if we can given any very clear picture of these effects at present. A sexual ethic founded on biology and on observation is probably far more capable of accepting such advances without the individual and social convulsions which have accompanied past revisions of ethics, than any system of absolutes.

Unlike the coercive view of marriage, the humanistic interpretation of sexual ethics is sufficiently elastic to cover the variations in person and circumstance with which it has to deal. Moreover, such judgments as it gives are amenable to arguments based on evidence. Religious codes have persistently asserted that certain responses and actions were always and at all times sinful or inappropriate. We tend now to limit assertions of value to one: that nothing, in any field of human conduct, should knowingly prejudice the welfare of others; beyond that point, it is likely that the use of psychology and biology as sources of standards will widen both the comprehension of the public and its power of solving a given emotional problem. Instead of asserting that extra-marital intercourse is always and at all times wrong, this system of ethics points out the responsibility of an individual to his partner, his children, and the third party, and leaves the exact pattern of his answer to his own social sense. This is a moral method that involves more individual hard work, and it has no magical power of generating responsible conduct – neither has the orthodox system of sexual ethics. Its prospect of success depends upon the fact that however much we may distort our standards in our own interest, conduct can at least be approached on this view at a reasonable level. The wife who has a lover, or the husband who has a mistress, are probably (in modern English society) not enjoying the simplest form of sexual relationship, though they may be adopting the most feasible and desirable solution for their particular needs, and any complications involved are a measure of their difficulties. These difficulties may inevitably include some injury to feelings, but they need not include guilt, anger, and outraged social dignity, nor the need to make, at any cost, the appropriate social gesture.

In fact, a good many marriages, and a good many personalities, require an 'adulterous' prop to keep them on their feet. This need may be 'immature' but it is certainly widespread, and it seems inevitable that our culture, like so many others, will come to admit and accommodate it.

Romantic love, as we have said, places a very heavy strain on marriage. In choosing a partner we try both to retain the relationships we have enjoyed in childhood, and to recoup ourselves for fantasies which have been denied us. Mate-selection accordingly becomes for many an attempt to cast a particular part in a fantasy-production of their own, and since both parties have the same intention but rarely quite the same fantasies, the result may well be a duel between rival producers. There are men, as Stanley Spencer said of himself, who need two complementary wives and women who need two complementary husbands, or at least two complementary love-objects. If we insist first that this is immoral or 'unfaithful', and second that should it occur there is an obligation to each love-object to insist on exclusive rights, we merely add unnecessary difficulties to a problem which might have presented none, or at least presented fewer, if everyone were permitted to solve it in their own way.

The balance of evidence seems to suggest that traditional patterns of sexual conduct aggravate associated difficulties rather than reduce them, and that personal conduct, being the concern of persons, is best regulated, even in its difficulties, by the judgment of persons, however fallible or injudicious they may be. The power of prohibition to make men good is something sociology consistently fails to detect.

NOTE

Page 108 – 'Adult fostered guilt and anxiety . . .'

We have direct evidence of the effects of pathological forms of religious teaching upon adolescents. Hunt (1938) records the story of a group of schoolboys who were exposed some to homosexual play of various kinds, others to revivalist religious conversion of a highly 'sin-conscious' type, and others to both these influences. In later life, all of the third group, but none of the first two, developed mental illnesses based upon ideas of guilt – some became ill only after many years. The effects of this type of emotionally determined religious instruction have obvious importance, both for educators and for religious youth-workers. (Hunt, J. McV. [1938], *Amer. J. Orthopsych.*, 8, 158.) Few 'pornographic' works can have done as much psychiatric harm as the literature on hygiene and 'clean living' which was formerly distributed to schoolboys.

V

Law and the Pattern of Sexuality

Most of the older political philosophies have a fairly clear-cut conception of the function of law. They regard it as the means by which individuals are restrained from behaving anti-socially, by the threat and exercise of punishment. This conception involves two assumptions: that individual conduct can be determined institutionally, and that punishment is effective in preventing anti-social behaviour in adults. Both these assumptions are now subject to very grave criticism from social psychology, and from common observation. If incest were lawful, it would probably be no commoner: if adultery were unlawful, it would probably be no rarer, only better concealed. The attitude of law to sexual conduct is, however, rather a special case in our own society. While there is no ground for assuming that imprisonment or the infliction of pain are conspicuously more successful in reforming non-sexual delinquents than they are in dealing with sex offenders, most non-sexual crimes are recognizably harmful to society, or to at least one class in it. By contrast, a very large number of sexual offences, including those most commonly prosecuted, are devoid of any recognizable social content, while many kinds of irresponsible sexual behaviour are not punishable at law. While, therefore, penal methods generally are facing increasingly severe criticism in terms of medical knowledge, there is something far closer to unanimity among doctors in regarding our sexual law as one of the most irrational and uncivilized features of our society.

There are two kinds of sexual offence which are punishable

in our culture: delinquencies with a sexual content, such as rape, and offences against social custom. We have seen how greatly Western civilization restricts the range of sexual activity which it regards as permissible, and in discussing the legal manifestation of this restriction we can recognize that many of the prohibited manifestations have simultaneously acquired the status of offences at law. Beside admittedly anti-social activities, there is a debatable body of practices, such as incest and abortion, which have social significance, though not in the same way that crimes of violence have social significance; their prohibition depends upon the attitude of our culture rather than upon the real effects of these actions; in the case of homosexuality between adults, however, or of offences that arise from the Western reaction to public nudity, the entire reaction of the law is dependent upon an exaggeration of a cultural attitude, and the arguments by which it maintains its position frequently appear as rationalizations.

The importance of the legal attitude depends, from our point of view, upon its capriciousness, its severity, and the frequency with which the sexually atypical individual finds himself in court. It is possible to recognize three main types of sexual behaviour which have serious social repercussions: irresponsibility of personal attitude, which is not a crime; general disorders of social conduct, expressing themselves in crimes of sexual violence; and sadism, a deviation of impulse that has far-reaching effects in non-sexual behaviour. A study of sentences imposed by the courts in the last two groups makes it clear that the severity of the punishment is generally proportional to the sexual content of the offence rather than to the damage it does, a system that is particularly undesirable in tending to wink at non-sexual, but socially mischievous manifestations of sadistic aggression.

Many sexual offences certainly incur exemplary punishment, and a great burden of public disgrace is added to the legal penalty. It might be inferred that this severity would be reserved for the most obviously damaging sexual activities – in fact, the savagery of the punishment is very nearly inversely proportional to the mischief done.

We can form some idea of the actual situation of the law, and its effects, from these facts. A very large proportion of sexual offences is accounted for by conduct which is socially atypical rather than socially destructive. In England and America the bulk of convictions in this specifically atypical group are for homosexuality and for exhibitionism. Three groups of individuals may be charged with sexual offences: delinquents whose delinquency happens to be sexual; clinically psychopathic subjects who fall foul of social custom; and individuals who, while not demonstrably psychopathic, are detected in some form of inacceptable sexual activity. The first group, which includes sexual assaults of all kinds, is very severely dealt with, but the severity is mainly directed at the sexual character of the offence rather than at its social gravity – a sexual assault with violence generally receives a longer sentence than assault committed in the course of robbery. Paradoxically, in the case of assaults on children, the legal proceedings and the attendant domestic uproar often do far more harm to the child than the original assault. Having been merely frightened, it is made to feel contaminated. The second group is variously treated: exhibitionism, in the form of indecent exposure, is possibly fortunate in being tried before a magistrate rather than a judge, the higher courts being far worse informed and far more prejudiced in their attitude towards psychological offenders than the lay Bench. Where psychiatry is made a condition of probation, it is handicapped by the repercussions on the patient of a public charge, which may make it necessary for him to change his work and his address, and which make him an object of persecution by his neighbours. Cases which are dealt with by simple punishment do even worse – twentieth and thirtieth convictions for indecent exposure are far from rare.

The third group is composed almost wholly of homosexual cases. It is in this group that the law acquits itself worst, because of the severity of the sentence, the social irrelevance of the offence, the frequency with which it is prosecuted, and the intensely emotional attitude adopted by the judges. It is also the group of offences whose treatment by the law has incurred the severest medical criticism in recent years. While, therefore, the legal attitude shows little evidence of change, we are probably approaching the time when pressure of scientific opinion may make itself felt in legislation. A recent official inquiry in Britain (1958) reported by a majority that homosexual behaviour between consenting adults should cease to be an offence. No doubt in time it will, after a few hundred more lives have been ruined by inquisition and imprisonment. It is a pity that we cannot hasten the process. With such a change in prospect it is important that psychology should press not only for change but for the right change – not all the types of reform which find advocates today would prove themselve in practice.

Older systems of psychology grouped all the odd and unacceptable manifestations of sexuality as psychopathies (basic disorders of personality): we now tend to regard them as variants, some of which are symptoms of personality disorder, while others, whatever their origin, co-exist with a reasonably good social adjustment. The distinction is important, since, from the psychiatric viewpoint, there is little point in devoting time to prolonged treatment of those conditions unless they handicap the patient or harm other people, and indiscriminate substitution of segregation and treatment for punishment is no solution. Added to the very poor prospect of success which attends the treatment of a resentful patient who has a genuine grudge against society, the recognition that a very large proportion of the public are capable of casual or occasional homosexual activities, any of which may conceivably land them in court regardless of the background in which they occur, makes the idea of psychiatry as a panacea for sexual variants unsatisfactory. At the present time homosexual behaviour between adult males by consent is treated by the courts on exactly the same basis as homosexual rape, and the punishment is identical for both parties.

The 'causes' of homosexuality are almost certainly environmental, though many constitutional factors may contribute to make a given individual sensitive to environmental pressures. The older conception of a 'third sex', having recognizable physical characters and existing as a compact entity has no

basis in reality. Homosexual behaviour is commoner in identical
than in fraternal twins[57] – like most other indices, from believing
in God to voting Conservative or developing short-sight – and
is to this extent 'constitutional' but the constitution which
predisposes to it in one country or age might equally well pre-
dispose against it in another. A. E. Housman's analogy to
hair colour is therefore quite inexact. A homosexual phase at
adolescence is common if not general in males and may persist
into adult life. 'Homosexuality' in the sense of sham mating
between males, is widespread among mammals other than man.[6]
In general, a preference for sexual relationships with members
of the same sex may represent the result of persistent Oedipal
anxieties, or a 'situation neurosis', depending on the individual's
failure to establish a proper relationship with the other sex, or
both. The shift of emphasis is not always a radical one, since a
high proportion of individuals are able to exhibit both homosexual and heterosexual conduct under suitable circumstances,
or in cultures which permit this. The fact, however, that a conscious and overt pattern of reponse implies a stable psychical
state makes psychiatric treatment less likely to succeed than in
cases where a homosexual 'way of life' is not systematized. One
result of the mixture of 'justice tempered with ignorance and
prejudice' which manifests itself in the legal attitude[42] has been
a defensive propaganda by homosexuals in favour of their
rights, based on a sense of separateness, and even an assertion
of superiority of feeling or aesthetic sense. The existence of this
attitude, and the burden of fear and guilt which is induced by
fear of prosecution and by a struggle against inner compulsion,
coupled with the high incidence of blackmail, also contributes
largely to the difficulty we experience in trying to modify
homosexuality by treatment.

We have to recognize that while the behaviour of the predominantly homosexual subject in our culture is often a
symptom, though it may be the sole symptom, of neurosis, the
attitude of society as exemplified in the courts is itself a neurotic attitude. The fact that it is statistically certain that some,
at least, of the judges passing sentence have themselves had
homosexual experience has been extended to suggest that

much of the reaction evoked by the whole issue depends upon the repression of homosexual memories and impulses in the public at large. If all psychopathies are suitable for compulsory treatment, then the anti-sexuality of English and American cultures, which is itself a deviation, falls in the same category and should benefit by similar treatment.

In dealing with homosexuality the main task at present seems to lie in stressing the potential presence of this pattern of conduct in a high proportion of males, and its lack of social importance even in individuals where it predominates: in other words, it is at worst an illness and at best a socially irrelevant preference. One frequent rationalization of the legal attitude takes the form of a conviction that any adult who exhibits homosexual behaviour, even if he is detected only on one occasion, is potentially delinquent and likely to assault or seduce children. This view is entirely unsupported by facts.

> Recent popular publications have left the impression that any homosexual may become a public menace as he grows older because of tendencies to attack children. There is no evidence which indicates that homosexuals harbour such potentialities any more than any other group of men. The pattern of sexual adjustment established early in life is likely to be maintained. If a man is attracted to adults he will continue to be thus attracted. A man who is conspicuously attracted to children merits continual observation and psychiatric investigation.[42]

Assault on children is an important social menace, because of the evidence which suggests that those who are assaulted in this way may in turn re-enact their experience later.[43] This, however, may equally well apply to heterosexual assaults, which have been known to lead to subsequent behaviour disorders. In a substantial number of cases, the child seduces the adult. The law as it stands fails to provide any safeguard, since there is also evidence that much of the mischief results from the attitude of adults to the assaulted child and from the ordeal of testifying in court. To such an experience the normal child reacts by fear and distaste; the most damaging element, that of mystery and contamination, is a product of our social attitude rather than of the offence, and adequate sexual education is probably the best protection for the child. The true importance of homosexuality in such cases is put in better perspective when we read Kinsey's pointed remark that if all American males who exhibit homosexual behaviour at some time in life were to be treated according to the letter of existing law, a majority of the male public would be in prison, and the unimprisoned would would be rather too few in number to staff the penal institutions which would be required to hold them.

It is probable, although the event seldom arises to test it, that almost any atypical sexual conduct, even if it occurs in intercourse between married persons, could be punished by existing English law. In point of fact, action is not taken against any but male homosexuals and persons detected committing incest or bestiality, a numerically unimportant group in criminal statistics. There is, however, another large group of offences originating in social custom which arises from the inacceptability of nakedness. Exhibitionism is a clinical entity, but it does not appear to occur in cultures that tolerate nakedness, even if only to a degree which allows the growing child to satisfy his curiosity. Such harm as the persistent exhibitionist does results from the attitude of his audience rather than the essential character of the offence. In another context of custom he might be an object of ridicule rather than of fear, and those individuals whose income and intelligence permit them to veil their abnormality under a guise of hygiene and nudism attract little attention. While the public attitude towards the homosexual is stubbornly resistant to scientific change, the prohibition which produces both the exhibitionist and his outraged audience is vanishing quite fast from the nursery and the home: so much so that some enthusiastic amateurs of psychology are now inclined to force the pace and object to signs of body-shame in their young children – forgetting the place which anxiety over the configuration of man and woman seems to play in normal instinctual development: it would be interesting to hear an informed and moderate psychoanalytical view of family nudity in upbringing (not that 'nudists', 'naturists' and the like, or their activities, are generally morbid – clothes have been the chief symbol of sexual inhibitions ever since Genesis, and their removal figures frequently in dreams as a token of emancipation: formalized nudity is therefore a lay sacrament with a healthy cathartic value, quite apart from being pleasurable: a psychoanalytical case has lately been made for adult nudism as tending to reduce the unconscious tendency for man and woman to view each other as no more than animated genitalia with a person secondarily attached to them, which goes with an exploitive sexual attitude). It seems likely that in any culture where the naked body is an emotionally charged object, exhibitionism will tend to occur in those who are still psychically infantile. Exhibitionism requires treatment today apart from any social repercussions, if only because it may become a major disability. It is accessible to psychiatry, especially if taken early and if the patient has not been brought before a court.

There are several similar deviations which may not be recognized for what they are: hair-cutting, ink-throwing, and so forth. In these cases the unrecognized 'case' who is treated as a nuisance and fined, escapes the fate of the more obviously sexual offender, because he does not arouse the prejudices of the court; he is likely, however, to offend again. Very nearly all these offenders, so far from being aggressive enemies of society, are ineffectual individuals who have been forced by their ineffectuality to return to the earliest and least adult forms of self-gratification. They are inmates of the nursery rather than the penitentiary. The law, unfortunately, still treats them by increasing their guilt and diffidence, exactly as it treats sadists by hanging and torture, or homosexuals by segregation in a homosexual environment. Viewed dispassionately, these anachronisms in the reaction of the law, particularly in view of its supposed functions of protection and reform, are worthy of the Mad Hatter or the King of Misrule, with the difference that unlike these the law possesses both the will and the power to impose itself upon society.

One peripheral manifestation affecting legal status which is wholly new, and which is due largely to the advance of plastic surgery, is the outcrop of cases in which adults 'change their sex'. These individuals are either intersexual in their genital characters, genetic females with markedly over-developed male characters due to adrenal virilism, or – perhaps most commonly – genetically and physically normal males who are homosexual travestites, and who have succeeded in talking a surgeon into sharing their conviction that they are 'females imprisoned in a male body'. The possibility of radical alteration of the genitals by simple joiners' work is something new to man, and comes dangerously near the longstanding fantasy-reactions toward intersexuality which seem to underlie many curious ethnographic findings, particularly the traditional genital mutilations; a similar group of fantasies is not rare in schizophrenia. The whole question of sex-change raises some nice problems in medical ethics. Some would blindly reinstate the chromosomal sex, some the sex, if any, in which the patient is likely to be fertile, and others the gender role which the patient chooses. From this point of view it is highly important to realize that the gender role and the physical makeup in man are almost wholly dissociable – a child brought up in the contrary sex, even if physically normal, is fixed in the learned gender role by the age of 18 months to 2 years, after which it is too late to make a change with impunity. This remarkable observation is itself important as an answer to those who persist in representing homosexuality as a matter of hormones – it is doubly important that practitioners should realize it in dealing with children of doubtful sex. Requests for such surgical 'reassignment' may also be made round about puberty by the patients themselves – often as the culmination of a long period of uncertainty about their true gender. In these cases action may be justified – what is probably never justified is to force an arbitrary reassignment against the established gender role, for this will be retained, and the result will be an artificially-produced homosexual.[64]

PSYCHIATRY AND THE LAW

The distinction between such obvious sexually-motivated offences and 'ordinary' crimes has been stressed in order to get treatment for those whose behaviour is inexplicable in terms of

conscious motive – but actually the lawyers who insist that
there is no such difference are often right, though for the wrong
reasons. Everyone now recognizes compulsive hair-cutting or
shoe-stealing as the mark of a 'case'; compulsive stealing by
the respectable (i.e. the prosperous and articulate) is coming to
be similarly recognized. But the motives of ordinary burglary
often are equally sexual – though the thief steals objects of
value, sells them, and has clearly a pretext intelligible to us
all for doing so. The same applies to dangerous driving, fraud,
and a whole range of aggressive or antisocial behaviour. The
attempts of the law to go beyond overt fact-finding and assess
the part played by 'guilt', i.e. avoidable and purposive misdeed
at the conscious level, and the Freudian underworld of compulsions which helps to make one man a judge and another a
housebreaker to satisfy a similar inner compulsion – these attempts wear thinner and thinner every year. A book on sex is
not the place to deal fully with penal reform; but the lack of
real distinction between obviously irrational and apparently
motivated crime is worth making. The punishment of the
sexually deviant who happen to express their deviation in
sexual behaviour is only a special case, a starting-point towards
the rational investigation of all offenders. Not all have predominant unconscious motives – but many have.

Discrimination by the law against offences having a sexual
content is by no means new: in Chaucer's time the ecclesiastical
judge under his canon jurisdiction —

> boldely did execucioun
> In punisshinge of fornicacioun,
> Of wicchecraft, and eek of bauderye,
> Of diffamacioun and avoutrye ...
> And eek of many another maner cryme
> Which nedeth nat rehercen at this tyme;
> Of usure, and of symone also:
> But certes, lechours did he grettest wo.[14]
>   'The Friar's Tale.' 2–12.

The history of this emphasis is traceable, as we have seen,
from primitive through Hebrew, Roman-Christian, and later

patterns of culture; its persistence in criminal law represents the end result of a prolonged struggle between the doctrine and attitude of Western culture and the biological demands and lapses of the individual:

> The methods of legal control of sex expression have varied widely . . . the doctrine behind the law, the doctrine of sexual morality itself has varied not at all. The doctrine is the doctrine of chastity which was developed by the early Christian fathers out of the customs of primitive peoples and out of their enunciation in ancient Hebrew law . . . to which English law has sought again and again to give expression for English peoples.[44]

The unreasoning severity of this system of legal attitude is directly traceable to the older pattern of asceticism and anti-sexuality, persisting in fields where it has succeeded in enforcing itself. It has been expelled from other fields by the impossibility of enforcement; as late as 1875 attempts were still being made to make adultery and extra-marital intercourse into punishable offences. Laws of this type remain in force in several of the United States of America, but, as in the case of the Cromwellian code, which prescribed death for adultery, they have remained dead letters almost from their enactment,[53] there being a limit to the compliance of juries. The field of legal control over sexual manifestations is, therefore, not the outcome of any conscious consideration of the needs of social protection; it is determined by the persistence or non-persistence of a public attitude condemning the offenders and upholding the laws and their sanctions. At hardly any point in history have the laws effectively determined, or, to judge by their frequent re-enactment, significantly modified, the pattern of sexual behaviour. Even in the minority whose conduct is reprobated both by the law and by social attitude and practice, it seems likely that the effect of statutory prohibition is to insure secrecy rather than abstinence, although the timid may be deterred.

One of the factors which makes modern judges distrustful of psychiatry (there are others, but this one probably stands high on the list) is the feeling that, once permitted to intrude an inch into law, medicine will take an ell – in the words of one barrister, 'that there will be nobody left to punish'. Judges tend to see themselves as guardians of society not only against crime, but, less consciously, against changes of custom and standard. The psychologist who points to the non-achievement by punishment of the ends which it is supposed to be seeking may easily be depicted as a sentimentalist who prefers the criminal to society whereas, in fact, it is often the exponent of punishment who prefers his own emotions to the purpose he is pretending to serve. It is fairly clear that if social medicine continues to advance at its present rate, there will in fact be nobody left to punish, since the best method of approaching the delinquent will be determined increasingly by examination of the results rather than by emotions and traditions. The fact that psychology calls in question the whole penal system does not, however, disqualify it from suggesting modifications. We do not have to endorse imprisonment as a treatment for non-sexual crimes in order to point out its singular inappropriateness in most sexual offences. Accordingly, a wide section of legal and medical opinion (including a special committee of the British Medical Association[45]) has come to demand specific changes in the law: among the suggestions have been the establishment of an age of consent for males, and the retention of two wide categories only of sexual offence – assault and the seduction of minors, of or by either sex; and conduct alarming or annoying to the public. It is thereby recognized that sexual conduct which does not affect society is not the concern of the law; the behaviour of consenting adults is their own business, so long as they behave with suitable decorum and restraint. This represents the legal position in almost all civilized countries except our own, the Communist *bloc* and the United States. But in recognizing this as an immediate objective, we have also to recognize and admit the artificiality of the line which divides sexual from non-sexual delinquency. Neville George Heath was as much a criminal psychopath when he repeatedly posed as an officer as he was when he committed the murders for which he was hanged. The fetishist who steals shoes is set among the goats; if he removes his trousers instead, or even as well, he is one of the psychiatric sheep. It is legitimate to suggest that while a reform of the law may prevent the continued persecution of sick men, it will not be adequate until our penology is sufficiently rational to be able to detect and treat the Heaths of society at a far earlier stage in their career.

The judges are also on firm ground in disliking the possibility of indefinite detention upon medical opinion. Any decision to confine anyone in an institution requires safeguards at least as robust as those of England's Certification Laws, and there is a real risk that a partial reform of our present sexual laws may lead to the lifelong segregation of individuals who do not 'respond to treatment' and who exhibit homosexuality as their sole abnormality of conduct. The point of real importance in any attempt to press for reform is that we are dealing not merely with mistaken beliefs but with social customs and attitudes that are themselves manifestations of neurosis. The homosexual and the exhibitionist are patients persecuted by other patients. The literature of the hundred years preceding the coming of psychiatry reflects a violent oscillation between emotional fear of perversion and an equally emotional defence of abnormality as an intrinsic good; as with all the other problems which sexuality poses in society, the main educative task is one of emotional deflation, the letting in of sense and study to replace stereotyped responses. Like other cultures, our own selects the forms of abnormality and anti-sociality which it will tolerate, and which it will punish. In our laws, as in our society, the sexual manifestation of abnormality is penalized, while its manifestations in power, greed, or irresponsibility are compatible with our standards. In the law itself, and particularly in debate upon the desirability of such punishment as hanging, flogging, or torture, delinquent impulses may be as strongly entrenched as in the criminals recommended for such treatment, and the unconscious motivation of much punishment is very clearly revealed by a study of newspaper correspondence in such debates. 'Still less different from born criminals are those latent criminals, high in power, whom society venerates as its chiefs,' wrote Lombroso. The real *point d'appui* of reform is the attitude of the individual and of society, and this can be reached only through education based upon fact and objective study. Reform of the law may be desirable or essential, but to break down the isolation of the individual, to increase the tolerance of society, to remove fear, to foster biologically reasonable living, and by these means remove the causes of imbalance while we reform its treatment – these are the primary objectives.

SOCIAL ASPECTS OF SEXUALITY AND THE LAW

The law, beside taking cognizance of sexual variation, affects sexual conduct in attempting to regulate social behaviour generally. I have not discussed the question of legal marriage under this head, because marriage is more readily studied at its personal and individual level, and because legal restrictions upon such personal conduct are decreasingly potent in determining behaviour. Incest more properly falls under the heading of sexual deviation, although the prohibition against parent-child incest is much more deeply rooted in human character-formation than the prohibition of homosexuality; we need to recognize this origin, since the biological arguments based on effect upon progeny no longer command acceptance;* in our society, one might expect that the psychological effects upon the participants and their children might well be serious, though the event is not rare. Brother-sister incest is commoner still – far more so than is generally realized, both among children and, occasionally, in adults.

The other specifically social prohibitions deal with prostitution, abortion, and sexual discussion – the last of these has been dealt with already in discussing censorship – and attempts have been made to introduce laws regulating artificial insemination. Legal prohibition of contraceptive appliances and of prophylactics against venereal disease persists in some countries.

---

* Close consanguinity over several generations is likely to cause the appearance of harmful recessive genes, but a single mating of this kind is not more likely to do so than a cousin marriage, and less likely than repeated cousin marriages. The 'inadvertent incest' argument against A.I.D. is therefore magical not biological. Even the close endogamy of many Indian castes has apparently caused little loss of vigour.

In our own, they are subject to a fair degree of underhand official obstruction.

> Mr. Kenneth Robinson (Lab. St. Pancras N.) asked the Minister of Health if in view of the high rate of induced abortion among married women and the large numbers of unwanted children coming into public care he would urge local health authorities to tell mothers, through health visitors and by any other means, of the availability of family planning services.
>
> Mr. Powell: 'No, sir.'
>
> Mr. Robinson: 'Is it not a ridiculous position that even where family planning clinics are held in local authority premises, it is forbidden to advertise them or publicize them in any way? Is it not time that the Minister ceased to be intimidated by a religious minority from adopting a rational policy towards what is a most valuable and necessary health service?'
>
> Mr. Powell: 'I am not intimidated by anybody (Government cheers), and I do not accept that the existence of these facilities and their availability is not well known or that doctors, where they consider pregnancy to be undesirable on medical grounds, do not refer their patients to the necessary advice.'
>
> *The Guardian*, May 15, 1962

Some of these prohibitions belong to the same category as sexual censorship, in being manifestations of a cultural bias, but others, such as the prohibition of abortion or brothel-keeping, raise more interesting issues. Prostitution being generally admitted, since the days of white slavery and abduction, to be an evil, the law claims to be fulfilling its function in attempting to prevent it, and the measure of its success or failure is largely a measure of the efficacy of law in general; similar issues are raised by the wartime attempt to provide compulsory treatment for venereal disease.

Promiscuity (or its opposite) is a custom: prostitution is an institution, that is to say, it involves a relationship which is exploitive on both sides, but in which the rules are known, and the possibilities of misunderstanding correspondingly reduced. The financial part of the transaction is only essential in that it is the chief guarantee that neither party is misinterpreting the situation. Other cultures have had other socially-approved signals to indicate the same thing – a casual sexual relationship which both parties fully intend to be such. In resorting to a prostitute the client knows (1) that he will get, approximately at least, what he wants (2) that time and money will not be wasted on social preliminaries appropriate to a different situation, and (3) that there will be no social come-back, no attempt, that is, to transfer the relationship to another level, and no risk of being misunderstood.

Beside being an institution, prostitution is a way of life which is actively chosen; under modern conditions in England, where there is no 'white slavery' and little direct economic pressure from poverty, the choice is usually quite deliberate. So far as our society is concerned, this choice implies a definite personality disorder – the whore, however, is only very rarely the oversexed heterosexual 'wanton' of the religious stereotype. Her main attribute is often defiance, and the sexual component of her activity is a means to an end, not the reason she chose it. The end itself is harder to determine – it may superficially be the 'good time' of folklore which lures girls to ruin. Intelligent girls may indeed achieve a 'good time' of this kind, but usually as demi-mondaines and mistresses in whom the law has no interest, not street-walkers. Much more often it seems to be the desire for a condemned occupation as a gesture of aggression against society or against parents. The prostitute of literature is an extraordinary and misleading example of masculine fantasy – so far as modern England is concerned she bears no resemblance at all to the real thing. One can imagine such a person – half mother-figure, half fantasy-fulfiller, the boundlessly permissive if fickle woman, with india-rubber emotions one cannot injure and an insatiable but complaisant physical appetite: now and then one meets her in real life – but in our culture she does not become a commercial prostitute. Possibly in nineteenth-century Europe she may have done – but judging by modern versions, the literary evidence is suspect. She ministers to the most cherished of all male fantasies – that of the permissive, sexually aggressive 'playmate'.

Fantasy, however, helps to keep the real whore in business. Many of the boys who talked to Kirkendall[28] had visited one, on the instance of friends, so as not to be thought 'chicken' – all had been disappointed or repelled – and all had boasted to their friends of the ecstasies experienced. I strongly suspect that the same happens to older men. The cultured and elaborate hetaira, of course, does better – she is much nearer to the reality of the dream. But if we knew more about the professional's clients I think we should find that most of them were disappointed pursuers of an unrealistic fantasy.

The emphasis placed by revolutionaries and philanthropists upon the economic origins of prostitution is misleading, so far as present-day England is concerned. Low standards of living may add a financial incentive or operate by creating mental stress, but recent theory places the emphasis rather on conflict and bad environment during childhood, and on the presence of immature or regressive patterns in the personality of the prostitute. Usually she is someone who rejects men rather than someone who cannot resist them. Prostitution is, moreover, the overt outcome of many factors, and its practitioners can be divided into a number of groups. Mercenary wives and 'gold-diggers', while not technically prostitutes, may exhibit similar patterns of motivation. Emotional problems, low intelligence, frigidity, unconscious homosexuality, and regression are prominent in English and American prostitutes of the street-walking variety, who are those chiefly singled out for legal persecution.[22] For these reasons, neither punishment nor the doctrine of inevitability could really be expected to assist our approach to the problem. The most important prophylaxis, not so much of 'prostitution' itself, as of the remote patterns which make some people practise it, lies in early recognition of insecurity in childhood, and adequate investigation of girls who exhibit the syndrome of truancy, pilfering, and maladjustment; experience has shown that the provision of security and stable affection can prevent the further systematization of this pattern, provided that it comes early enough, and before the victim has incurred any serious social consequences. In adults, psychotherapy, ranging from suggestion to analysis, can do something to help the patient, though the fully developed psychopathic prostitute is not an easy subject to help, and intelligent prostitutes have been known to attempt the conversion of the psychotherapist. The moral indignation of courts and respectable citizens is 'a positive encouragement to recidivism';[33] bearing in mind that frigidity rather than lust, and a basic incapacity for normal personal and sexual relations, is the commonest stigma in contemporary prostitution, argument based on moral reform is singularly unprofitable.

Public-health experts and moralists have debated the best institutional approach to prostitution for many years, one school advocating prohibition while the other pointed to the impossibility of enforcement and proposed a supervised toleration on the European model. The facts which appear today lead us to a rather different approach. The causes of prostitution as we now have it can be studied; they are sufficiently evenly distributed between individual environmental factors, providing the supply, and social factors, providing the demand, to require very widespread changes in our cultural pattern as a part of any remedial programme. The forms of action open to the law are therefore palliative. But it is typical of the weakness of institutional reform that neither of the proposed remedies, suppression or toleration, can in fact be implemented. Suppression has been rejected, in its fullest form, because of the manifest impossibility of enforcing institutional measures without the support of public standards; the same consideration has modified the form of our laws against drinking and gambling, but it is beginning to apply to less contentious fields; the discrepancy between the law and the current standard of honesty is increasingly quoted by judges. Regulation has proved equally impracticable for the opposite reason: it offends against a long-standing cultural attitude and encounters vocal opposition from a minority which probably enjoys fairly widespread public support, apart from any scientific arguments against such a toleration. Since the Street Offences Act we have therefore settled for rather shamefaced persecution designed to drive matters underground where the righteous will not be obliged to see them. Prostitution provides a striking example of a socially and psychologically emotive evil which cannot be attacked by any orthodox institutional route; the legal system which attempts to palliate by prohibiting solicitation settles down to an irrational equilibrium with public practice, in the periodical prosecution of prostitutes; and in the desultory harrying rather than the prohibition of their activities. Meanwhile the increase in promiscuity has gradually shifted the emphasis away from its original focus, the professional prostitute, who is a denizen of relatively stably constituted cultures.

In point of fact, the best way of dealing with prostitution might well be to improve the standard of entry to the profession. Although its association with psychopathology makes it a valid medical problem in our society, with the sole exception of venereal disease all the 'social evils' of English prostitution today are the direct results of our valuation of it. At a time when Puritanism forbade music and stage plays, there was a strong tendency for actors to be rogues and vagabonds, recruited by necessity and irregularity rather than talent. Even in living memory one motive for embracing the arts has been a desire to spite one's relatives and scandalize the respectable very like that shown by the prostitute in choosing a condemned occupation. No doubt psychologists in a music and theatre-hating society would describe, quite validly, a specific psychopathology of entertainers which made their profession a social evil – under such conditions the standard of their performance would be correspondingly low. As soon as these activities acquire prestige and cultural acceptance they change their personnel – the quality of entrants becomes higher, and in time the maladjusted individual with the right talents is counselled to take up music or drama as a means of acting-out. There is, indeed, a characteristic personality-defect behind many successful actors, but they are able to use their chosen activity for our benefit and for their own.

This comparison is not flippant. It is really impossible to talk of a psychopathology of prostitution *in general* because that institution has, and has had, different valuations in different cultures. In Ancient India the social valuation of the prostitute was almost exactly that which we accord to the dancer or the concert pianist who renounces domesticity to be a virtuoso artist (which she often was). Often the occupation was heredi-

146

tary, from mother to daughter. If sexual virtuosity were to acquire a different valuation in our society the 'problem' of prostitution would disappear, and its personnel would change very markedly – in particular, many of those who now constitute an offence to society by being prostitutes would have to find other ways of offending it.

Another legal impasse arises over the suppression of abortion. In this case, we are dealing with an important cause of premature death in healthy adults, and with the extortion of money from people in trouble, but neither of these dangers is diminished by institutional action; in part, the original problem, which originates in the inadequacy of contraceptive instruction and in the social status of illegitimacy, is actually aggravated by laws which drive the practice of abortion underground. The prohibition is circumvented by those who can afford it, while those who cannot are exposed to the extremely grave physical risks of 'back-street surgery', as well as to blackmail.

VI

Remedies and Methods

As sexual sociology has derived its information from a wide range of studies, it draws on an equally wide range of activity and method in putting the results of those studies to remedial use. Any system of hygiene which begins with the need to bring about far-reaching changes in conduct, whether those changes involve diet, sanitation, or sexual behaviour, has three main outlets for its teaching: thought, institutions, and individual counsel. By far the most important is the influence which new ideas exert on the intellectual climate of the time: general public education of this kind, and the bringing of contemporary thought into line with the results of investigation, takes place largely at second hand and slowly; much of the work of the conscious educators consists in correcting misstatements and extreme statements, but it is in this field that the scientific study of sexual ethics has produced its most far-reaching social effects. General exposition of this kind is the proper field for debate and the stating of personal viewpoints. The second educational vehicle, the use of official and institutional means of propaganda, has a limited value in such fields as the prevention of venereal disease, but the general structure of authority, and even of non-governmental institutions such as the school, is itself often too inimical to the principles which sociology wishes to inculcate to be of great service. The co-operation of governmental mechanism has, in general, proved dangerous to the spread of rational ethics, and the structure of our society makes it very likely that it would be particularly dangerous to rely on such co-operation in attempting to modify socio-sexual patterns; institutions are too concerned with self-defence against the attacks of rational investigation to be useful allies in their own modification. The third remedial method, that of direct psychiatry, must therefore provide the other main vehicle for the application of our ideas. The change of atmosphere represents improvement in living at drawing-board level: psychiatry is the repairs service. It is being developed in a growing range of forms, from the treatment of general psychical disorder to the more limited work of adult sexual education and marriage guidance. It is easier to theorize about society than to apply theory to the individual in the way which will benefit him most: while general theory is the place for strong personal opinion, psychiatry is under an obligation of compromise in the interests of the patient.

In other words, we can modify social attitudes by public discussion based on fact, and we can answer individual problems by a graded application of general principle to individual cases. For the first of these activities we need a certain freedom of public discussion and an accessibility of the public to scientific ideas. Both of these are present today. For the third, we need a large number of adequately informed and selected medical and social workers, who will become available only with the spread of newer social ideas into the medical profession and the medical curriculum.

In dealing with marriage, we have considered some of the answers we can give, on a basis of knowledge, to individuals who ask for scientific guidance. Anyone who takes this advice seriously will, however, very rapidly discover that he cannot carry it out, because the social pattern in which he lives will interfere perpetually in any attempt at reorganizing his way of living. At the crudest level, one cannot rear children 'in a stable home environment' if one is going to be put in the street by the landlord as soon as pregnancy becomes evident; one cannot develop happy marital relations if one is to be conscripted and sent abroad, or unemployed and anxious or compelled to live at close quarters with in-laws for lack of a house. At the subtler level one cannot easily be mature and secure in a commercially competitive society where nobody knows his neighbour, and where nuclear war is round the corner. Nor can one expect to be happy, permissive and adaptable if one has been reared by parents who laboured under these social handicaps.

The remedies are accordingly political, but politics is becoming a branch of psychiatry – some would say of applied psychopathology. The earliest psychiatrists, concerned with the illnesses of individuals, increased their knowledge of human conduct as they treated sick men. Once a scientific investigation of any field of human activity is fairly under way, there is no return to the state of thought which preceded it. From the study of the sick man, social psychology has grown, rather like Jack's beanstalk, to a point at which neither its practitioners nor the public can ignore its final implications. The individual who cannot live in terms of modern mental hygiene, because society prevents him, recognizes that the study of individual problems leads ultimately and logically to the modification of society. The political method, if by that term we mean the method of social change which has figured in every previous statement of social objectives, itself comes under the scrutiny of new ideas and can no longer stand up to this scrutiny. Political systems of theory not only reveal a far larger proportion of unconscious motives and of rationalizations than any world theories except those of religion: they also, by the insistence with which they base themselves on the belief that human beings can be socially reorientated only if they are institutionally governed or directed, run counter to much that is now known about the motivation of conduct. To these systems social psychology opposes a method which is in line with the general pattern of science. It attempts to define the desirable form of society by studying the ascertainable requirements of individual happiness and normality, and the means of attaining the necessary change by studying human conduct and the forces that determine it. To this extent, scientific sociology 'supersedes' politics, exactly as epidemiology supersedes magic as a means of abolishing malaria and smallpox: it does not supersede individual and group action in defence of the 'life centred' values and ends which politics as now practised ignores.

I have worded this claim as belligerently as possible, because, as we have seen, scientists, and medical scientists in particular, have a well-founded horror of expressing their findings in political terms, which arises partly from a dislike of the irrelevant uproar of social change, and partly from a fear of contaminating rational methods with the prejudices that attend political attitudes. But it will be plain from what has gone before that a statement of the desirable pattern of individual conduct makes nonsense without an extension of the description to cover the type of society in which such conduct is possible. The psychiatrist who treats sick individuals and the social psychiatrist who may ultimately influence sick societies are clearly members of an identical scientific project.

It is already possible to give a tentative picture of the direction in which our ideas of such a society are moving.

> We begin to get a picture of a country with a scanty, scattered population, neither concentrated in great towns and cities nor spread quite evenly over the land as in a primitive farming community . . . here meeting for some functional, productive purpose, there subordinating productive purpose to psychological considerations . . . a decentralized and 'demechanized' community which nevertheless makes full deliberate use of machinery and technology to serve its purposes.[46]

The objective is a society different from any previous anthropological pattern, as hygiene differs from the normal distribution of health, because it is the objective of conscious planning rather than the outcome of cultural and natural forces. If we look closer at the presuppositions which sociology is making in detailing this society, we shall see that they are these: the chief export and manufacture of such a society is to be health, or, if we prefer it, the values of life for its own sake; it must combine the entire range of potentialities which exist in technology and in the machine with some of the aspects of primitive cultures which are biologically necessary – the term 'paraprimitive' has been coined[46] for this combination, to distinguish it from back-to-naturism and from purely mechanical and 'productive' patterns; it must be based on the exchange of personal responsibility which goes by the name of mutual aid, and its cohesion and order maintained by the attitudes of its individual members, and not by any system of institutional power as we now know it. It abandons the view of human misconduct as the product of something immutable in the individual which requires to be suppressed by force from without as a condition of public order. If the suppressive view of sociality were correct, any attempt to institute a desirable society would depend primarily on the restriction of anti-social conduct, by means of coercive powers vested in authority. And in this case, we should be perpetually exposed, as we are today, to the risk that these powers will fall into the hands of individuals who are themselves anti-social in their predominant attitudes, a risk which becomes a certainty when we consider the association which exists between anti-social impulses and the desire to dominate others. The balance of evidence appears to be tilting steadily against this view of the suppressive function of society. The view which makes it possible for us to accept the possibility of superseding politics by scientific method, rather than reject it as a psychological version of perpetual motion or squaring the circle, is that the whole of human conduct, desirable and undesirable, rests on a balance between a self-assertive impulse and an impulse which we can reasonably term love. 'It is solely due to the extraordinary fact that love gratifies selfish needs in the course of unselfish behaviour that any satisfactory solution can be imagined.'[46] Society is seen as a medium for the expression of the social, 'loving' impulse, depending upon the cultivation of this impulse rather than upon the repression of its antithetic partner.

We know also that where anti-social impulses predominate, severity is usually quite incapable of modifying them, beyond the doubtful achievement of making them secret or transferring them, unaltered in their essence, to a permitted field such as war, power, or competitive exploitation. The present age is an age, in England, of very depressed revolutionaries. Revolution in its nineteenth-century significance, a mass movement of the people against a particular institutional system and in support of another, seems farther off than ever it has been. The depression of those who wish to revert to this pattern of political reform is fully justified. So is the depression of those surviving enthusiasts who hope to abolish cancer by means of amulets, or malaria by purifying the air. That the application of sociology to life will involve 'revolutionary' action by the mass of individuals, which may prove at least as strenuous and exacting as that envisaged by the older revolutionaries, should not be allowed to obscure the difference between the new and the old.

I cannot discuss in full the basis of the new idea of sociological revolution (it is not really new – the guesses of former anarchists and liberals have simply received confirmation from social science); an excellent exposition of it has been given in the book by Taylor[46] from which I have quoted. But it will be obvious from what has been said about the formation of character that for those who accept this view education assumes a very much greater importance than it has ever held in the eyes of the institutionalists, because the degree to which sociality can manifest itself in the adult is known to depend upon the relationships that exist in the family, and between the child and society.

In the particular facet of reform that deal with sexuality and sexual ethics, educative work predominates – including, of course, the unlearning of a good deal which has been long hallowed by tradition. Education is of two kinds: the help we can give to the child, and the treatment – for it is, in fact, treatment rather than education – we can give to the adult. It is probable that the attitude of any individual towards sexuality, as towards other social activities, is so firmly determined by the age of sixteen or seventeen that attempts to change it in adult life must depend as much on 'treatment' in its wider sense as upon facts and argument, if the change effected is to be real as well as apparent. Such change can be effected; if it could not, we should be up against a vicious circle, since parental attitudes determine child education, and child education determines parental attitude in the next generation. One thing that can guide the approach to both forms of education is the close analogy that exists between neurosis in individuals and irrational patterns of belief in societies. We sometimes distinguish between character- and situation-neurosis, but both have a common element – they are patterns of rigid response to a given stimulus, as rigid as instinctive patterns in animals, but unlike instinctive patterns they fail to subserve a coherent function. Many are what animal psychologists would call a displacement activity. A neurotic reaction has as its main features rigidity (the same coin produces the same ticket when it is put into the machine) and inappropriateness (the ticket bears no relationship to the desired destination). Many of our stock responses which have passed, in former times, as instinctive, such as our violent reaction against sexually atypical conduct, are examples of socially subsistent neurosis. The process of placing sexual conduct on a reasonable basis is almost wholly concerned with the replacement of stock, non-valid responses of this kind, which are as valueless to society as a compulsion to count stairs is to the obsessional individual, with attitudes based upon the appreciation of facts and of realities. As the stair-counter is uncomfortable if he does not count, so the individual who violates one of these fixed patterns of response becomes uncomfortable as a consequence of his violation, and the particular discomfort which he feels takes the form of guilt. The detachment of guilt from sexuality, with which it has so long been associated, is the other prime objective of sexual education, and our success in achieving it depends on our success in altering the neurotic pattern.

Many able books have been written about the sexual enlightenment of children – recent workers are finding it necessary to emphasize that the infectiousness of parental attitudes is a more important factor than the imparting of fact, however essential that may be. It is virtually impossible to persuade a child by lecturing that sexuality is a perfectly worthy component of life, and that its exercise calls for the same reasonable restraint as other social conduct, if we ourselves are inhibited or irresponsible – even when our inhibitions manifest themselves in a preoccupation with sexual emancipation. Sex education, therefore, consists primarily in imparting an attitude by contagion, secondarily in providing factual instruction, and as a corollary of these, in tolerating the manifestations of sexuality in childhood and adolescence, giving such guidance as is necessary not only to see that they are harmless, but also that they are enjoyable. In these fields the individual can do much, though it is easy to underrate the difficulties and the social rebuffs which may result from misunderstanding by other members of society, and it is possibly harder to explain the need for tact than it is to cultivate the healthy attitude of the child. Intelligent parents already face a good many possibilities of friction when they give their children information which others withhold, or when they tolerate masturbation or other overt manifestations of sexuality in their own sons and daughters of school age. The success of sexual hygiene in altering the attitude of parents and teachers is far from complete, but its success has been striking, and since further progress can come only through individual persistence, the child and the parent must be fortified against the time lag that exists between individual and social approval.

The problems of the adult are identical with those of the child, but they are deeper ingrained. Our approach to the psychiatric side of sexual education brings us directly into the field of social reform and raises all the issues of principle which that extension involves. We have to consider our objectives and relate them to the immediate possibilities.

There is a strong case for a literature of sexual enjoyment which treats the elaboration of sexuality as Indian and Arabic works have treated it – at the level of ballroom dancing. Not that technique and elaboration can rid us of immaturities; still less are they a substitute for adult love. On the other hand, they can provide reassurance and pleasure, and heighten the element of play which, as I have already suggested, is perhaps the marker of good sexual adjustment, if not the cause of it. There are virtually no European works of this kind, for the tradition has not, until recently, permitted them – there are plenty of marriage manuals, certainly, but of a Stopesian squareness which is enough to make one abandon the project before the banns are up. Such books as there are have commonly been clandestine and eccentric – that of the Viennese medical gymnast Weckerle, which lately came my way, is a case in

point.[3] Gymnastic mats and a catalogue of 531 postural variants
notwithstanding, the sexual prescriptions of *The Golden Book of
Love* are surprising now, not for their oddity, but for the ex-
periential good sense they contain, and for the healthily un-
European attitude they adopt to the part played by sexual
pleasure and its elaboration in the good life. We have our
Lawrentian apologists for enjoyment as an inherent good, but
most of them strike us forcibly as people who have had no such
satisfactory experience themselves. Elliot Paul once tried to get
it written into the law that would-be censors in Boston should
produce evidence of satisfactory sexual experience. The same
should apply to the writers of books on the art of love. Weckerle,
it appears, was also a physician – if anyone frowns on this
brand of medicine, he had his answer from Avicenna – 'non
turpe est medico, cum de rebus venereis loquitur, de delecta-
tione mulieris coeuntis: quoniam sunt ex causis, quibus per-
venitur ad generationem:' writing about erotics is a perfectly
respectable function of medicine, and about the way to make
the woman enjoy sex; these are an important part of reproductive physiology.

Writers on political revolution tend to distinguish between
two types of attitude, the revolutionary and the reformist, by
which they mean the approach to a problem based upon the
acceptance of radical change, and the approach based on the
gradual pushing and pulling of existing institutions into the
desired form. A rather similar division exists in constructive
sociology. In educating the society in which we live, we have to
distinguish between objectives and palliatives. I have said that
an approach to sexual adequacy is only one facet of the approach to social adequacy, and that social change of the type
which recent work appears to favour must involve positive
solutions of the problem of power in society. This is both a
political and a sociological objective, and we are fully justified
in reasserting that attempts to secure such reform through the
existing mechanisms of government are likely to be a waste
of time, and to incur the same failure as that of the ideals of the
French and the Russian revolutionaries. The only intelligible
basis for social change lies in the modification of individual

attitudes and the encouragement of resistance to irrational authorities.

Where medicine and political sociology join, in the field of social psychiatry or of special applications like marriage guidance, we have to strike a far more difficult balance between objectives and palliatives. We cannot decline to help individuals to make the best of existing circumstances, and yet we cannot reasonably adopt means of palliation which aggravate the problem as we see it in general principle. The most satisfactory means of reconciling general objectives with practical possibilities undoubtedly lies in the fostering of individual experiments in social living within, and if need be in opposition to, centralized political patterns. This approach has none of the obvious defects of compromise, though groups of this kind cannot avoid the charge that they derive protection from the order they are attacking – there is no very good reason why they should not. Where they are recruited from adults brought up in the asocial tradition, they may prove strenuous to live in, or unintentionally comic, but such experiments have behind them a record of solid achievement which commands respect.

But the majority of those who come to us for advice will not be ready to burn their boats and join a resistance movement, either in society or in a limited field such as sexual ethics. Most of them have a positive adjustment in the society where they grew up. They cannot realistically be expected to abandon their own long-standing attitudes as readily as the Galilean fishermen abandoned their nets.

This is a problem that recurs throughout all psychiatric and advisory practice, and it explains the undesirability of zealots in clinical work – or, more accurately, of zealots who do not know when to abstain from pressing their own position, however sound it may be. The patient's own erroneous judgment, and his own irrational attitudes, demands as much respect from us as we would wish accorded to our own. For this reason, sexual education, in common with other forms of social psychiatry, is not a field in which one-track minds are desirable, whether we regard their particular direction as progressive or the reverse. The psychiatrist who assaults a lifelong Roman Catholic with denunciations of his irrational approach to sexual conduct is an ass. Argument, statement of personal attitude, and advice based on the adviser's own conscientious standards are all legitimate (they are the methods we should apply to convince an unbeliever in the truth of a chemical or a physical finding), but not the in-and-out-of-season preaching of a personal view, regardless of the patient and his context. There are authenticated cases where injudicious advice in such terms as 'Take a lover, you need sexual experience' has produced domestic uproar and a lowering of the credit of social medicine which was not prevented by the psychiatric soundness of the advice. We have to minimize the shocks and difficulties which the patient is going to experience. We may not always think it wise to destroy an entire pattern of adjustment to fit the theoretical plan. If some such radical action really is needed, we must not be frightened of it, but major redirection of social attitude is most satisfactorily accomplished outside the actual consulting-room. On the other hand, it often happens today that the patient is fully aware of the gap between his needs and the demands and opportunities of society, and it is here that social psychiatry has been far too hesitant, and far too ready to restore an adaptation which is, in essence, a step backward.

It is obvious from this that sexual educators need careful selection. One of the defects of much marriage-guidance work at present lies in the high proportion of advisers who enter it with the specific object of propagating a religious or a 'progressive' ethical system without due consideration to the patient. No adviser should advise against his own conscience (the judgment of this book that such a conscience should be based on rational standards is in itself an assertion of attitude, but one which cannot in this context be avoided); compromise with the attitude of the patient, coupled with guidance towards a more satisfactory attitude, is as necessary as it is difficult to achieve.

Yet another form of pressure we need to recognize is that which arises from the difference between social standards and customs in adviser and advised. Custom and moral judgment are so inextricably mixed, and so rooted in various social strata, that this is part of the preceding problem. Kinsey draws attention to the bewildering sequence of condemnation and approval which a child may undergo if it is caught at some socially unacceptable sexual practice. The boy masturbates in public: the policeman, coming from a group that regards masturbation as perverse, and tends to prefer pre-marital intercourse, takes a severe view of his moral deficiency: the juvenile-court magistrate may be the product of a group in which masturbation is regarded as normal: the probation officer or the remand-school headmaster may side with the policeman, and so on. If the 'offence' is sexual play with a girl of his own age, the victim's experiences may be reversed: the policeman, who did the same thing at the same age, may be forced to take action by the law: the magistrate may regard the child as an oversexed psychopath or a wicked hooligan: the psychiatrist, from another layer, will take yet another attitude. How far this is true of English society, which is perhaps less neatly stacked, one cannot say, but in all work where advice is given on sexual conduct class attitudes may intrude in a most unwelcome way. The readiness with which the 'poor' are shocked has always been a source of wonder to the charitable. The exact range of topics and actions which shock them differs considerably from that which shocks the bourgeois adviser. The sum of this problem is that there is no substitute in any form of psychiatry for a wide human understanding which accepts no general remedies and is properly and thoroughly informed. Doctors and clergymen seem to possess more than their proper share of innocence, with praiseworthy exceptions, and innocence is the last quality which is of value in giving advice to the sexually perplexed. Its possessors are very often as wise as doves and as harmless as serpents.

Innocence is, in this context, synonymous with ignorance. One of the really serious defects in contemporary medicine has been the gross inadequacy of the teaching of general psychology in medical schools, as well as of its special applications to sexual problems. The first is the more important, since it implies a widespread failure to diagnose psychological disorders, an equally widespread tendency to treat them by medicine or misplaced exhortation, and a very great difficulty, experienced even by highly intelligent students, in deciding, after qualification, what published textbooks of psychiatry they can regard as reliable. More important still is the failure to give the embryo doctor enough insight into his own attitudes to prevent him from acting out at his patient's expense. This is really being remedied only now, and only in some medical schools with lively departments of psychiatry. Sexual problems, with which we are dealing specifically here, would make up a larger part of the practice of the average doctor if his patients had any confidence in his qualifications to solve them. Those students who are accurately informed at qualification owe their knowledge to their own exertions in reading a literature that abounds with eccentricity and misstatement, and any insight they may possess to luck. Any newly qualified graduate of many a medical school who was confronted with say, a case in which homosexuality appeared as a problem, and who attempted to deal with it solely on what he had been taught, would be clueless and useless: he might recall from his forensic lectures that it was a criminal perversion, or he might have a vague idea that it required hormones or psychoanalysis; the wise would refer it intact to a psychiatrist and retain his feeling of achievement unimpaired, thereby avoiding a duty which a family doctor is particularly well placed to discharge. The unwise and arrogant would do a deal of harm through what Freud called 'wild' analysis. A married couple, both aged twenty-three, appeared at an infertility clinic. The husband was in a state of suppressed anxiety bordering on explosion. The wife complained of dyspeptic symptoms, treated with powder for two years. They requested immediate artificial insemination. It came out in the history that sexual intercourse had been abandoned after four attempts, and never renewed, in three years of married life. Two approaches to the family doctor had been rebuffed by him with the remark that he had no intention of starting a rubber-goods shop, and they ought to consult their parents. This is clearly an extreme case, but unfortunately such cases still occur, and lesser degrees of uncomprehension by doctors, or of ignorance even when the attitude was superficially sympathetic, have produced a deep-seated unwillingness in the public to consult them in sexual matters. This is certainly less pronounced than it was, but the forms of behaviour which are socially inacceptable are still far less commonly admitted to general practitioners than we know them to be in the statistical record, and most practitioners who are not psychiatrists know virtually nothing about the natural history of their patients' reproductive behaviour (by contrast, some of them are excellent, and much wiser than over-enthusiastic consultants).

Research and instruction in contraception stand high on the list of remedial activities which sex educators must undertake in their attempt to improve existing conditions. The biological and biochemical side of this problem has now almost been solved: a contraceptive which was harmless, stable, simple to use, and wholly reliable might well alter our entire outlook upon sexual ethics, and further research may at any time bring about this change of situation, if it has not already done so. With the methods at our disposal, we already have a large number of special problems to solve. Contraception has been misrepresented as a threat to the persistence of the 'intelligent classes' of the community, and a consequent danger to racial health. It seems likely that the decreased relative reproductive rate among families of high intelligence is a social phenomenon which could best be attacked by modifying the pattern of society; it is at any rate clear that the balance can be redressed only by making still easier contraception possible and available for less intelligent families, whose high fertility is not a matter of choice. The world food shortage, especially in Asia, has made contraceptive education in overcrowded areas a pressing necessity, but the attempt to introduce it encounters great difficulties. In areas such as India, illiteracy and custom are serious obstacles, and few methods depending on chemicals or rubber appliances are effective for mass use under tropical conditions.

'Control by men and women over the numbers of their children is one of the first conditions of their own and the

161

community's welfare, and in our view mechanical and chemical
means of contraception have to be accepted as part of the
modern means, however imperfect, by which it can be exer-
cised.' – Royal Commission on Population.

Contraception now plays an important, and beneficial, part
in our daily lives. Apart from those who object on religious
grounds, there are probably few married couples who do not at
some time employ it. But it is not true, as many unmarried
people assume, that there has existed 'contraceptive information'
which made it possible to avoid or space pregnancies without
difficulty, and without prejudice to coital enjoyment. Contraception by the best available methods, occlusive or spermicidal,
until the advent of systemic hormone analogues, was a nuisance
and often an anxiety. It could be practised with fair success, so
far as avoidance of pregnancy is concerned, by educated people
with good sanitary facilities, using it upon premeditated
occasions, but for the ill-equipped or unintelligent it was quite
inadequate. For quite a few women the manipulation necessary
for insertion of caps or suppositories is strongly distasteful;
anxiety over possible unreliability is a common cause of
frigidity; male methods may interfere considerably with
sensation – while both gasoline rubber and many chemical
contraceptives interfere with the normal genital odour, which
is a significant 'releaser' for many couples. Research on less
clumsy and more reliable techniques for controlling fertility
has had a recent impetus from fears about the world's food-
supply; and contraception is urgently needed to contribute to
the solution of this problem. But the tone of some 'neo-
Malthusian' comment merits the rebuke directed by James
Parkinson to Malthus, that 'if the population exceeded the means
of support, the fault lay not in Nature, but in the ability of
politicians to discover some latent defect in the laws respecting
the division and appropriation of property.' A more liberal
justification for contraceptive research lies in the part which a
simple and reliable method could play in extending human freedom of choice and deepening human relationships. The biologist who gives time to this problem need have no doubt that
he is meeting a universal human need and wish.

An ideal contraceptive should, in the words of Parkes,[47] 'be effective over a known period of time, simple enough to be generally available and easily usable by any people intelligent enough to know the possible consequences of coitus, and whether they do or do not wish to conceive. Ideally, it should involve only occasional dosage by mouth. It should certainly not depend on local action contemporaneous with coitus. It should have no other effects than the prevention of conception' – or, of course, prejudice subsequent fertility when discontinued. In seeking biological means of achieving this, attention has been devoted to three groups of substances: (1) anti-hyaluronidases, which interfere with the penetration of the ovum by sperms, (2) two materials which have been regarded as hormone antagonists – namely, extract of gromwell (lithospermum), which appears to antagonize the pituitary gonadotrophins, and *m*-xylohydroquinone. This second substance was identified by Sanyal[48] as the ingredient of oil of peas which reduced the fecundity of rats on a pea-meal diet, and it seems to antagonize vitamin E and to inhibit the actions of œstrogen and progesterone on the endometrium. Synthetic *m*-xylohydroquinone has had fairly extensive field trials in India,[49, 50] capsules being administered to women monthly at about the time of ovulation and it certainly appears to reduce fertility. (3) Hormone antagonists which interfere with ovulation, implantation or both – these are the most promising of all.[15] With contraceptives, though toxicity tests in animals can and must be undertaken, clinical trial on human patients, on a large scale, is the only final means of estimating efficacy and judging untoward effects on health, subsequent fertility, and any pregnancies which may occur in spite of the drug. In present circumstances women in Asia might well be prepared to accept some degree of risk if it freed them from the burden of child-bearing – often itself fatal. But most medical workers would hold that where calculated risks are taken they should in fact be calculated, and the calculation should include that of the patients.

The steroid contraceptives, taken by mouth, which either suppress ovulation or prevent implantation are the materials to which most workers now look for the best results. About two million women in America alone are now using these substances. (It would greatly simplify our assessment of any real side effects if medical men writing about these matters could be made to declare their religious affiliation – the 'pill' may have real drawbacks, though no insuperable ones have yet appeared, but there are already signs of an organized whispering campaign to scare off the public by hints about cancer and deformed babies – there are none so unscrupulous as the devout.)

However, local action on the sperms, either before or after they leave the male, may eventually be preferable on general physiological principles to alteration of the female endocrine balance. (Some of the methods that have been proposed, such as the use of œstrogens to induce tubal spasm which will imprison the ovum, seem to offer possibilities of mischief; and one material tested did in fact produce abnormal fœtuses.[52]) The main trouble with male methods is the refusal of males to use them: they should perhaps be advertized as aphrodisiacs for prestige reasons. Among the more familiar expedients improved occlusive tampons suitable for use under tropical conditions offer at least a partial protection, and work on these is going on. Recent improvements in rubber lubricants and in thermal properties of rubber have made the condom a far more satisfactory proposition than it was a year or two ago (it is the teen-age method *par excellence*) and it commends itself, particularly in countries where contraceptives still have to be smuggled. Immunological methods of inducing 'hostility' to sperms of a given father have so far progressed little, and would probably fall in the category of 'luxury' contraceptives. It is the poor man (or woman) under bad conditions who most needs and desires an advance in biological methods of controlling fertility. We should work more systematically to provide it for them. Both in quantity and quality, past research left a lot to be desired, and the 'disreputability' of contraception still anachronistically limits the number of first-rate workers.

Attention should be drawn, however, to an aspect of this research – or rather of public reaction to it – which is seldom mentioned. The people of some Asian and African countries, though they want contraceptive facilities as a right, have reservations which in their position we might share. Any suggestion that 'the West' was trying to produce a substance with which foodstuffs could be doctored and the fertility of Eastern peoples reduced might release a reaction far more powerful than the Indian Mutiny precipitated by the use of pig grease on cartridges. Such suspicions have been voiced; they have all the psychological attributes of an ideal rumour; and unguarded remarks about the beneficial effects of radiation in lowering the population of the world (in countries other than that of the speaker) may lend colour to them. For such reasons the spirit in which biologists and doctors approach this problem, and their motives in working on it, may be as important to their ultimate success as is their technical proficiency. If, as many believe, we are developing in contraception a human right and a human freedom, it will do no harm to say so fairly often.

The moral and social importance of contraception in our own society, even in view of the imperfections of existing methods, is that it introduces into sexual activities an element of choice which no previous culture has enjoyed. It removes a compulsion – which is why it is so alarming and threatening to religious ideologies which depend on the maintenance of sexual guilt. Its potentialities for the growth of the aesthetic and personal aspects of sexual culture depend on the success with which we manage to reform and modify the social background; in a world where responsibility is penalized, or where war and insecurity remain endemic, it may easily provide the means by which the individual expresses his protest; infertility under present conditions has some of the qualities of a strike against urban asociality. But anyone who has observed the effect of the fear of unwanted pregnancy on the mental and physical health of overworked mothers will be unlikely to underestimate the benefit, in increased security and increased control over individual and family living, which cheap and simple contraception provides. Voluntary control over conception is a feature of our lives which has come to stay, and which is now fortunately beyond the reach of prohibition though not of obstruction and misrepresentation; its risks are no different from the risks which come from other advances in human control of environment, and like these other risks they can be met only by social education in a biologically and mentally tolerable environment. The opposition to contraceptive education has much in common with the opposition to the control of venereal disease. Both appear to have been motivated in part by fear of the withdrawal of any check or drawback to the enjoyment of sexual relationships – pregnancy, like syphilis, has for centuries been one of God's sanctions against lust, effective where superstitious awe has failed to override biological and instinctual drives.

If fertility can be a cause of problems, so too can infertility – indeed, almost every gynaecological clinic seems to house two queues of people, one seeking contraceptive advice and the other complaining of infertility. Some but not all of the infertile can be assisted to conceive naturally, and others will eventually do so. The number of frustrated couples would be cut considerably if those who want children would make a point of having them early, before subfertility intervenes. For the others, there is now the possibility of insemination, either with a concentrate of the husband's semen, or with that of someone else. Hudibrastic scruples have been raised in some minds over every stage of this process by the professional manufacturers of sexual anxiety[61] – even the use of the husband's semen has been attacked if it has to be obtained by masturbation! – at the same time, physicians have been pardonably inclined to go slow, for fear that deepseated human reactions might be aroused by any process which tampered with the parental sense of achievement and 'own-ness' in the children. Doubters expected that the already disturbed might be the chief applicants for donor insemination. In fact, follow-up studies show a rather better level of parental adjustment in such cases than in the average process of marital reproduction – far better than among applicants for adoption, many of whom require exclusion as would-be foster-parents because they manifestly intend to use the adopted child as a medicine or a missile in a pre-existing marital problem. As so often happens in sexual matters, the public is displaying more commonsense over donor insemination than the tribal medicine men – or, for that matter, those eugeni-

166

cally-minded biologists who talk at large about storing the semen of men of genius so that all our women can father Lenins and Einsteins. It has been gently remarked by one of America's most eminent geneticists[62] that we might not want a world peopled largely by Lenins and Einsteins, even if that were likely to result from such substitution – which it is not.

The training of personnel and the provision of education for the educators are clearly among the most urgent tasks in social medicine. The ideal counsellor, if we constructed him to specification, would need to be a superman – he would require a stable personality and enormous personal experience of life, psychiatric training to give him insight and enable him to impart it, or know when to abstain from imparting it: a biological training to keep his psychiatric methods on the ground and related to physiology and mammalian origins: a lack of axe grinding intentions coupled with a revolutionary fervour for better things – in fact, a Frankenstein whom we are fortunately unlikely to be able to produce in bulk. Accordingly we must make do, in medical education, with fallible but reasonably well-balanced individuals who have a smattering of these attributes, plus a great deal of intuitive liking for, and judgment in dealing with, their fellows. This is a compromise between what Michael Balint has called the 'two medicines' – the rigorously rational and the interpersonal, which is the root of good doctoring. The advance which has been made, and which is particularly evident in sexual education, has to be maintained on so wide a front, and in such a range of fields, from individual psychiatry to political sociology, that every part of our life and society comes under scrutiny. It is also increasingly obvious that unless theory can be translated into individual action, and that very quickly, we run the risk of total cultural collapse through war, the fear of and preparation for war, or a general loss of nerve. The most dangerous current attitude is that which accepts the impotence of the individual to modify the course of national policy, or even of his own life. We all know that revolt may be a reaction-formation, that those who rebel, even against social forces which there are rational grounds for rejecting, may be unconsciously motivated, and that there

are risks in endorsing 'rebellion' without further particulariza-
tion. Unconscious forces are present in all human activities.
In reasserting the responsibility of the human being for what he
does, psychiatry is nevertheless faced at times with the need
for something very like deliberate subversion. In the context of
social psychopathy, disobedience to irrational attitudes and
directives acquires the status of a positive social value. We are
prepared to recognize this in discussing the disobedience of the
individual to such directives as those given by Hitler to the
C.O. of Belsen, but we are less ready to accept the need for a
similar watchfulness in the context of our own society. The
deterioration of Western pretensions during the war, which
culminated in the atomic bomb, points to the unreality of such
a distinction between democracy and totalitarianism. A conflict between sociology on one hand and the traditional mechanisms of government on the other was always foreseen by the
earliest believers in the theory of the free society, who tend, like
Godwin or Kropotkin, to talk in terms of nineteenth-century
revolutionary action. The likelihood of such a conflict remains,
unless social sciences are themselves captured by the mechanisms of power and rendered subservient to them. It is plain that
such a revolution cannot usefully be envisaged in the military
terms which appealed to some, at least, of the earlier revolutionaries; it is more likely to follow upon the collapse or the threat-
ened destruction of the existing patterns under the weight of
their own contradictions.

It is difficult to predict the 'future course of society', and the
event usually surprises those who try. At the moment we have
not only the advantages and drawbacks of extremely rapid
rates of change, but a frenzy of motivation – where the motives
lie we may guess but cannot prove – which has made knowledge
grow exponentially through scientific and technological research. This exponential growth can hardly go on for ever – it
must eventually flatten out, to give place, perhaps, to a more
relaxed and less motivated society which will rest on its oars
and devote more time to the enjoyment of living for its own
sake, a skill we have almost lost. In such a society contraception and a loss of anxiety over sexual matters generally may

mean that erotic interests, which are after all the most psychologically and physiologically appropriate source of 'kicks', will replace not only the adventitious excitements we now pursue, but a fair part of individualistic art and the whole of residual religion, as well, perhaps, as a large part of the 'drive' behind modern technological progress. Unwin[37] is empirically right, to the extent that permissive societies are not as a rule very original or progressive; our sons and daughters may be willing to accept this for a few generations at least, in exchange for the advantages of not being hell-bent on anything. Even the emotional relationships in such a society might look shallow to us – but our intensity, mirrored in plays and fiction, will look as irrelevant to them as King Oedipus' overreaction to a pardonable mistake. A less intense world might, indeed, be no bad thing.

With the development of the social sciences, man is presented with the opportunity of attaining his adulthood. At present it appears as if humanity, by intensive effort and conflict, is only now at the point of reconciling its technological achievement with the type of social living that is sometimes approached by primitive societies, we have the problem of getting both 'togetherness' and technology, both mutual aid and modern medicine. The mapping and claiming of this heritage is the joint responsibility of science and of the individual. The struggle against unreason, against death, and against power is the concern of psychology and medicine, because it is the concern of man. It may be that in the liberation of family and sexual relationships lies the dynamic by which that struggle may be brought into a victorious issue. The good life, as Bertrand Russell has said, is inspired by love and directed by intelligence. There is no field in which this is more true than in our sexual relationships.

References

1 Sinibaldus, Ioh. Bened. (1642) *Geneanthropeia, sive de hominis generatione decateuchon.* Rome.
2 Lorand, A. (1925) *Old Age Deferred.* New York, F. A. Davies Co.
*3 van Week-Erlen T. (Weckerle, J., psued.) (1907) *Das goldnes Buch der Liebe,* 2 vols. Vienna, p.p.
4 Bromley, D. D. and Britten, F. H. (1938) *Youth and Sex: A Study of 13,000 College Students.* New York and London, Harper.
5 Davis, K. B. (1929) *Factors in the Sex Life of 2,200 Women.* New York and London, Harper.
*6 Ford, C. S. and Beach, F. A. (1952) *Patterns of Sexual Behaviour.* London, Eyre and Spottiswood.
*7 Freud, S. (1929) *Introductory Lectures on Psychoanalysis.* 2nd edn. London, Hogarth Press.
*8 Fénichel, O. (1954) *Collected Papers.* First Series. London, Routledge.
9 Székely, L. (1957) *Int. J. Psychoanal.,* 38, 98–104.
*10 Lampl, H. (1953) in *Drives, Affects and Behaviors.* New York, University Press.
11 Hutchinson, G. E. (1959) *Amer. Nat.* 93, 81–91.
12 Comfort, A. (1959) *Amer. Nat.* 93, 389–391.
13 Comfort, A. (1961) *Darwin and the Naked Lady.* London, Routledge.
*14 Kinsey, A. C., Pomeroy, W. P. and Martin, C. E. (1947) *Sexual behaviour in the Human Male.* New York, Saunders.
15 Devereux, G. (1951) *Psychoanal, and Culture,* 1951, 90–107.
16 Ouspensky, P. D. (1932) *The New Model of the Universe.*
17 Becker, H. and Hill, R. (1948) *Family, Marriage and Parenthood.* New York, Heath.
18 Dickinson, R. L. and Beam, L. (1931) *A thousand Marriages.* Baltimore, Williams and Wilkins.
19 Hamilton, G. U. (1929) *A Research in Marriage,* New York, Boni.
*20 Terman, L. M. (1938) *Psychological factors in Marital Happiness.* New York, McGraw-Hill.
21 Halliday, J. (1946) *Lancet, ii,* 185–191.

References

22　Glover, E. (1945) *The Psychopathology of Prostitution*. London, I.S.T.D.

23　Wilson, J. G. and Prescor, M. J. (1949) *Problems of Prison Psychiatry*. Idaho, Caxton.

*24　Lorand, S. (ed. 1949) *Psychoanalysis Today*. London, Allen & Unwin.

25　Fowler, W. C. (1947) *Lancet i*, 273.

26　Mackenzie, I. F. (1947) *Social Health and Morals*. London, Gollancz.

*27　Westermarck, E. (1922) *The History of Human Marriage*. London, Macmillan Co.

28　Kirkendall, L. A. (1961) *Premarital Intercourse and Interpersonal Relations*. New York, Julian Press.

*29　Flugel, J. C. (1921) *The psychoanalytic Study of the Family*. London, Hogarth Press.

30　'*Teenage Morals*'. An Education Pamphlet. Education Press Ltd., London.

31　Hammond-Tooke, W. D. (1962) *Bhaca Society*. Oxford, Univ. Press.

32　Herskovits, M. J. (1938) *Dahomey*. 2 vols. New York, Augustin.

33　Hogbin, H. I. (1946) *Oceania 16*, 185–209.

34　Strain, F. B. (1943) *Sex guidance in Family Life and Education*. New York, Macmillan Co.

35　Bradbaart, S. (1961) *Lancet ii*, 764.

36　Eyles, L. (1947) *Commonsense About Sex*. London, Gollancz.

37　Unwin, J. D. (1933) *Sexual Regulation and Human Behaviour*. London, Williams & Norgate.

38　Mace, D. (1943) *Does Sex Morality Matter?* London, Rich & Cowan.

39　Way, L. (1949) *Man's Quest for Significance*. London, Allen & Unwin.

*40　West, D. J. (1955) *Homosexuality*. London, Duckworth.

41　Allen, C. (1958) *Homosexuality: its Nature, Causation and Treatment*. London, Staples Press.

42　Henry, G. W. (1948) *Sex Variants*. New York, Hoeber.

43　Mackwood, J. C. (1947) *Med. Press*, 5652, 217.

44　May, G. (1930) *Social Control of Sex Expression*. London, Allen & Unwin.

45　*The Criminal Law and Sex Offenders* (1949). Report of a Committee of the British Medical Assn.

*46　Taylor, G. R. (1949) *Conditions of Happiness*. London, Bodley Head.

47　Parkes, A. S. (1953) *Proc. Soc. Stud. Fertil.*, *5*, 20.

48　Sanyal, S. N. (1955) *Int. med. Abstr.*, *16*, 91.

49　Sanyal, S. N. and Ghosh, S. (1955) ib. *18*, 101.

References

50   Sanyal, S. N., Banerjee, S. C. and Sen, J. (1955) ib. *18*, 31.

*51   Pincus, G. (1963) *The Future of Man*—CIBA Fdn. Colloquium. London, Churchill.

*52   Zuckerman, S. (1956) *Nature*, Lond. *177*, 58.

*53   Tanner, J. M. (1962) *Growth at Adolescence.* 2nd Edn. Oxford. Blackwell.

54   Greenacre, P. (1953) *Psychoanal. Child Study 8*, 189–194.

55   Greenacre, P. (1955) ib. *10*, 184–194.

56   Jones, M. C. (1957) *Child Devel.*, *28*, 113–8.

57   Kállmánn, F. J. (1952) *J. nerv. ment. Dis.*, *115*, 283–298. *Amer. J. hum. Genet.*, *4*, 136–146.

58   Hailman, J. P. (1960) *Amer. Nat.*, *93*, 383–4.

59   Klopfer, P. (1959) *Ecology 40*, 90–102.

60   Comfort, A. (1960) *Lancet ii*, 107–111.

61   Schellen, A. (1957) *Artificial Insemination in the Human.* London and Amsterdam, Elzevier.

*62   Dobzhansky, T. (1962) *Mankind Evolving.* New Haven and London, Yale Univ. Press.

63   Mitchell, W., Falconer, M. A and Hill, D. (1954) *Lancet ii*, 627.

64   Money, J. (1961) in Ellis, A. and Abarbanel, A., *Encyclopedia of Sexual Behaviour*, art. Hermaphroditism. New York, Hawthorn Bks.

*65   Kubie, L. S. (1948) *Psychosom. Med.*, *10* 95–106.

66   Spitz, R. A. (1953) *Yearbk. Psychoanal.*, *9*, 113–145.

67   Lewinsky, H. (1944) *Int. J. Psychoanal.*, *25*, 150–155.

68   Feldman, S. S. (1952) *Yearbk. Psychoanal.*, *8*, 172–189.

*69   Heron, A. (Ed.) 1963 *Towards a Quaker View of Sex.* London, Friends House

DATE DUE